MARK WILLIAMS
TAKING BACK AMERICA
ONE TEA PARTY AT A TIME

Edited by Holly Williams

© 2009, 2010 by Mark Williams

Souvenir Edition exclusively for

TEA PARTY EXPRESS III

MARCH 27 – APRIL 15, 2010   **JUST VOTE THEM OUT!**   www.TeaPartyExpress.org

MARK WILLIAMS

TAKING BACK AMERICA

ONE TEA PARTY AT A TIME ©

Published in the United States of America 2009 by MarkTalk.com under the original title:

"It's not Right versus Left, It's Right versus Wrong;

Exposing the Socialist Agenda"

ISBN: 978-0-578-03278-8

By Mark Williams

© 2009 - 2010

Williams, Mark Lawrence 1956 –

Second Edition / Revised 2010

Dedication and Acknowledgements

This book is dedicated to the United States of America and all those who cherish and protect her, and in memory of those who have laid down their lives for her.

It is also dedicated to those patriotic Americans who fight on the Home Front to turn back the tide of the Domestic Insurgency that has grasped the levers of power from the people and threaten to destroy this Nation by ripping the American Dream from our grasp. Those people are the *Tea Party*.

I would also like to acknowledge the many thousands of working stiffs, whether in or outside the home, who daily labor toward that American Dream and make this country great. That would include my mother, Carol, and father, Larry; and my grandparents and lots of other family (on both sides).

This book is also in memory of all the honest, working men and women who were abused, broken, and discarded by the sweatshops of Attleboro, Massachusetts and places like it even today, without regard to the languages they speak – The American Dream is universal. and within reach of all.

Thank you to my partner, co-conspirator and wife, Holly, for her support and enduring patience in working with the consequences of my Public School "education" (which left me with only a passing familiarity of correct grammar, spelling and punctuation) in the editing of this work into a readable form.

Mark Williams,

Chairman the Tea Party Express

Sacramento, California

Mark Williams addresses
fellow Tea Party Patriots

Highlights from Inside

Welcome to the future

In "Future Shock" Alvin Toffler asked the reader to imagine an entire society being plunged into a new reality. He used the example of the culture shock experienced by a traveler who encounters customs and societies unlike that to which the traveler is accustomed.

How that traveler copes depends on the severity of the difference and the traveler's own level of coping skills. Toffler then asks the reader to imagine an entire society; including its most dysfunctional and ill-equipped, being suddenly thrust into a whole new reality where familiar social cues are absent, institutions foundationless and ethics so fluid as to be undefined. The chaos and turmoil he predicted would be enormous, perhaps even fatal to that society – at least as those in it know, or knew it.

That was 1969; it is now 2010 and welcome to Toffler's example come to life, with much of George Orwell's earlier nightmarish visions included. You and I are part of not just a society but also an entire planet suddenly awaking to an entirely new world. It is a world as frightening as it is exciting and fraught with as much danger as it is blessed with opportunity.

This book is the first to address the issues raised not in lofty tomes or "wonkisms" but rather spoken from the plain-English perspective of a public school educated, middle-class professional, from a blue-collar background who has been a professional communicator for three plus decades.

This book could not be timelier! The entire nation is engaged in vigorous debate over direction, the two major parties over their own directions and Americans are befuddled in their efforts to make sense of it all. I try to help you sort it all out and arm you with what you need to see through the lies and come join in saving America from the domestic enemies who occupy her corridors of power.

Much of what I have to say I learned from you; on the radio, in person, in correspondence and just watching you make the American Dream unfold every day.

Protecting our heritage and her promise is now on our watch and together we will not fail the ghosts of the Founders, surely watching over us.

"I am not an African-American; I am Lloyd Marcus, AMERICAN!

The Author

Mark Williams is the recipient of a *"Mark Twain Award"* from the *Associated Press Television and Radio Association of California-Nevada*, several lesser recognitions and has been previously part of journalistic teams that have won a variety of other awards including the Edward R. Morrow.

Mark Williams is a former director and vice-president of the *National Association of Radio Talk Show Hosts* and is a founding member of the Tea Party movement as well as Vice Chair for *Our Country Deserves Better PAC*, a Sacramento-based political action committee dedicated to defending the American Ideal and the chief sponsor of the Tea Party Express, chaired by the author.

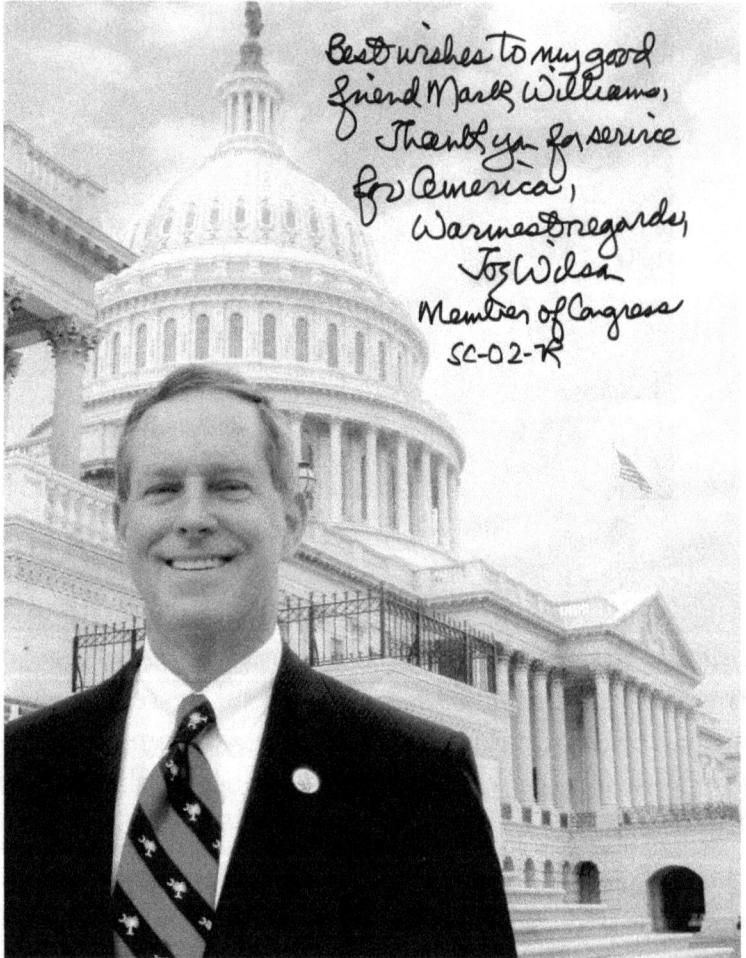

Congressman Joe Wilson (R-SC) who famously stood up during President Obama's 2010 State of the Union speech and shouted "YOU LIE!"

Why I Tea Party

I owe this country a lot. I am successful – frequently in spite of my own failings, but in any event only because I am a member of the Lucky Sperm Club and born an American. I was also lucky in that I was born into a time when being politically active was simply part of what Americans did.

In the South, Hosea Williams (no relation), Dr. King, and other icons of the Civil Rights Movement were facing nail-studded baseball bats and vicious dogs being turned on them by police. The crime? Marching for Civil Rights, Human Rights granted at birth by our Creator and for the first time in Human History enumerated and enshrined by fallible American hand, on fragile parchment.

A decade later in the North, the Athens of the East – Boston – became a bloody battle ground following a court order to forcing schools to enroll based on race and the wholesale busing of children for the purposes of desegregation.

In between and concurrent was Vietnam. Hardly a pair of decades to sit and remain uninvolved, even for this youngster, especially in an activist household.

But I was born a lower caste American and will never escape that label, yet only in America may someone from my (and my wife's) blue-collar lineage do more than dream, let alone actually achieve dreams. It is my mission to put my years of experience as a community organizer, activist, and journalist (teller of the story from a well-defined and stated point of view) to work on behalf of my nation – again.

During Vietnam, I was opposed to the war, despite being too young to enlist or be drafted. Yet so committed was (and am) I to the ideals of this nation that I preemptively enlisted in my own *"national service"* and spent my 14-18 year old summers as a teachers' aide, working with underprivileged, inner-city, minority kids in the original Head Start Program.

In 2005 my wife, Holly, and I borrowed $20,000.00 against our home to go to Iraq and risk our lives to see for ourselves (and report) on the actuality versus what we saw on TV and in the papers.

As a kid myself I was as active as a kid could be in the Civil Rights demonstrations, such as they were up North in the day, and later as a student in Boston during the Busing Riots.

Since then I have turned hundreds of thousands into the streets to protest injustice or government dysfunction or – as frequently - to raise money for an abused kid, save an abused animal or simply address a wrong to be righted.

In California, I was a key player in the recall of hapless Governor Gray Davis and a champion of secure borders and the elimination of illegal immigration.

I am an American

A man named Richard Warren set foot on Plymouth Rock from a little ship called the Mayflower in 1620. He is my ancestor and 3 ½ centuries later I lived and worked in the Cradle of Liberty, Boston. It was there where this nation was born and where first blood was shed. I have stood on the very spot as well as at the foot of the graves of the five Boston Massacre victims who shed that first blood, to pay my respects. The first to die was Crispus Attucks, a black man – and one with whom I have had many one-sided conversations at the Old Granary Burying Ground at Park Street Church, taking us full circle as today as the man sitting in the White House holds that job probably more because of his skin color than any other reason.

I have shed tears in Washington at the Vietnam Memorial, the Korean Memorial, the WWII Memorial, and Arlington National Cemetery, among other sacred places in nearly every state. That all contributes to my being more than a little possessive of my heritage and this nation's legacy.

My country and all she stands for are being battered by the storms of change predicted by Toffler. His work forewarned me of this day and I have worked ever since to prepare for it; I am well armed and seek to arm you. This book is only the newest arrow in my quiver. I have filled this book with simple language and pop-culture references to help explain complicated ideas in commonly understood terms and metaphors as well as quotations from noted authorities to back specific points.

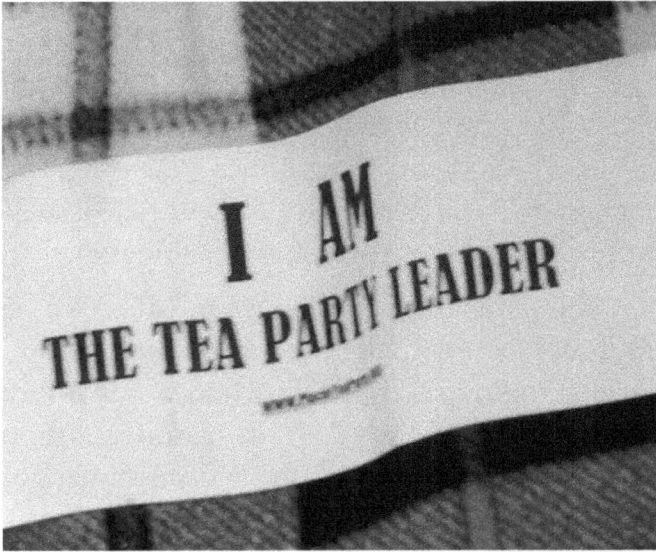

Saving America is your job and mine

"Somebody has to do something, and it's just incredibly pathetic that it has to be us."

Jerry Garcia, (of the Grateful Dead)

"When your opponent is holding all the aces, there's only one thing to do. Kick over the table."

Dean Martin as "Little John" in "Robin and the Seven Hoods" Warner Brothers, USA 1964

At first glance one is inclined to nod in agreement with the dead Dead Head but on closer examination Garcia demonstrates the Left's utter misunderstanding of the care and feeding of a democratic republic. For those who do understand America, Garcia unwittingly issues a clarion call more akin to Little John's way of thinking.

It is not *"incredibly pathetic"* that we should be the ones to *"do something,"* it is our obligation and duty as citizens to do exactly that! America was not designed to be run by "professionals." This nation was born of peoples who knew nothing other than professional governance and its associated dysfunctions and evils (in the form of royalty). In their experience the professionals held all the aces and what the Patriots who founded this country did was kick over King George's table.

While I would never suggest that you engage such an approach in a Vegas poker game, our experience today proves the wisdom of what emerged from the American Revolution, at least in terms of running a government. Look at the wonderful job that our present day, homegrown professionals are doing to us now. If that's "professional" I'll stick with the founding fathers and take rank amateur any day of the week and twice on Independence Day.

The very idea of America as guardian of human rights hangs on a slender thread of direct citizen involvement. As you read this book, what you will realize is the vast amount of damage done to our nation and her place in destiny by what I call the Culture of Non-Involvement coupled with the Culture of Dependency. The fundamental tenet of each is leaving it up to the other guy including forcing that other guy to provide for you and your family.

But before we break out the pitchforks, torches, tar and feathers there is a coup we must successfully pull off first. We must retake the Republican Party.

Those of us who share true Traditional American Values must regain control of the party that once was steadfast in its support and espousing of those values – the Grand Old Republican Party of Abraham Lincoln and Ronald Reagan. The values that you and I share may differ in precise detail but we share the underlying principles. We will likely argue over those precise details but not at issue are the ideas that underlie our belief in these ethics that also happen to be the only cure for what afflicts American politics and society today. The damage is severe but not irreparable. Together with like minds, you and I are going to see that the damage is repaired and America emerges even more assured of her true Manifest Destiny.

The GOP was born of the Abolitionist movement. Because the Democrats were steadfast in their embrace of slavery it fell upon those true to the principles of our founding to finally stand up for those principles. One of which is that humans are not property and that our Creator is blind to differences of skin color or continent of origin in assigning full human rights.

Upon the election of the first Republican President, a man from Illinois named Lincoln the Democrats declared a new nation. Consisting of states dominated and controlled by Democrats the new Confederate States of America (known as the Confederacy) thus declared war on the suddenly halved United States of America in defense of "property rights". The property in question being human beings sold by their own people to the Dutch, and then resold to American businessmen in both the North and the South.

Unfortunately today that champion of human rights and Traditional American Values is in disarray. The present day GOP is adrift, the moral and sensible rudder once carefully tended by those two great presidents (Lincoln and Reagan) now swings about wildly as the Great Ship GOP seeks direction and reason for being.

Leaderless, principle-less, and pathetic are just three of the words that I have been Cassandra-ing on the radio, on television and in this print collectively for nearly a decade in total now to describe the California and National Republican Leadership

Needless to say, my independent thinking and speaking of my mind has made me few friends among the Republican Party leadership, but then again I am an American and a Californian first. "Republican" is only my party affiliation and a fairly recent one at that. I pull no punches and I make no apology for my tone seen by some as "harsh," it is actually *"Tough Love"* and much needed Tough Love for a party and nation in crisis. I will worry about bruised feelings another time; right now my country is in danger.

2008 was my ninth presidential election vote and only the second in which I was not registered as "decline to state" (or "independent") although there has been the rare occasion when I have cast my vote for a conservative democrat and one, long-ago vote for Jimmy Carter, which taught me a lesson that I will never forget. From that point on as a young voter in Kennedy dominated Massachusetts; I *"wasted"* my vote on libertarians and independents more to my liking than either the predestined democrat *"winner"* or the traditional sacrificial republican.

As I moved about the country I listened, learned, and debated new and interesting points of view. The cumulative result is that I have walked a marathon in others' moccasins.

Now as all the "Arnold Schwarzenegger Republican" and George W. Bush chickens of destruction come home to roost, and our state and national future are in dire peril – all as predicted by this author and right on schedule – it is time for not just Republicans but all Americans to regroup and stage our own coup.

That's right, *"coup."* The election of Barack Hussein Obama was heralded as a "revolution" and indeed, it was. Even knowing that we have elected a man who holds offensive views that he is turning into policies which are the very antithesis to the very idea of America, it is nonetheless very difficult to not swell with pride at a nation that would risk its very existence to elect a black man president, perhaps more because of his skin color than any other reason.

That Obama was elected largely because of his pigmentation is not a difficult conclusion to reach given the void in Obama's words where substance should dwell. I believe that America was so hungry to prove the substance of our being that, provided with the opportunity, we blindly voted for a Holy Grail of a symbol knowing that the reality was questionable.

Just a brief blink of time in history ago this nation rounded up those who looked like (and sometimes acted like) the enemy. We then put them into internment camps in what we mostly agree now was a horrible - if necessary - moment in our history. Less than two decades later we ostracized and black listed people of all professions, including politics, who carried the dreaded label of *"communist."* Today we invite those who align with the enemy to occupy the corridors of power. Try not being proud of a nation as tolerant and good as to allow even evil the benefit of doubt as to debatable points! Maybe not so smart but certainly an inspirational leap of faith in the idea of reward for seeking human perfection that gives hope. Our challenge is keeping that hope from flickering out under the weight of what is now being called "Obama's Army."

The flag at our home flew upside down the day after Election Day 2008 because the statement had to be made but is right side up today because the man is unimportant. What is important is that this is not the first time America has risked her own life to rally around a symbol of our Creator-inspired embrace of human rights and equality.

Front lines

I know. In the 1970s, I was on the receiving end of some of those Molotov Cocktails and rocks being thrown in the streets of Boston, standing to protect little black kids on school buses being sent into hostile neighborhoods in one of the stupidest, most ill advised, forced integration schemes ever concocted. As foolish and destructive as it was there was no way that I, or the thousands in the streets with me, would stand for making those kids pay the price of a single judge's idiocy and the Neanderthal tribal response that shocked the Athens of America.

There I was, in the very same streets as our forbearers, engaging the direct defense of my Nation's honor almost 200 years later to the day suddenly realizing that the battle is never really won. We face an enemy that never sleeps. That which stalks our liberty is as indefatigable as it is insatiable.

It too is an idea, but not an idea that shall set you free. Quite the opposite in fact and it is on the defensive as We the People rise to meet the invader.

Nancy 'Hanoi' Pelosi occupies the Speaker's seat in the United States House of Representatives

Sarah Palin

T he professionals in politics and media completely miss the whole point of Sarah Palin's appeal as she electrifies those Americans who still understand their nation and their national heritage. It was Sarah Palin who tapped into our frustrations simply by being one of us, and gave us the real *"hope,"* of 2008 but could not overcome massive media propaganda machines like CNN and the New York Times in the election of 2008.

While conservatives lamented the erratic John McCain as the '08 GOP standard-bearer, he is only the symptom of the Beltway mentality. His instincts and connection with normal life are dulled from his years in the Congress then the Senate. It is simply not possible to live in that atmosphere for any length of time and not contract the self-serving and cynical myopia that is rampant in our Nation's Capital. Salvador Dali and Pablo Picasso displayed a firmer grasp of reality in their art, than do some them.

I knew the guy in the late 1980's and early 1990's. I first met him at the studios of KFYI AM in Phoenix where I was a producer and a host. A more normal guy you could not ask for as a senator. After leaving Phoenix I lived and worked briefly in Washington, DC at WWRC AM, where I lasted a whole 11 weeks for reasons that should probably be obvious. DC is not a town where people like hearing the unvarnished truth.

I spent some time on Capitol Hill. A couple of times I embedded with an elected official's office for a day at a time for a mostly off the record education as to the day-to-day operation of the building. McCain greeted me like an old friend and could not have been more…. well, normal I guess. With only brief flashes of the old John, the guy running for president in 2008 was not the old fighter pilot with a perfectly twisted and well-honed sense of humor and solid character that I knew from Phoenix and the Hill. He had become a satirical political caricature. As such he was seemingly uncomfortable enough in his own skin to conjure images of the invading interstellar "cockroach" character that hijacked the epidermis of Law & Orders' Vincent D'Onofrio, (playing the poor, farmer victim) in the 1995 comedy hit "Men in Black."

Sarah Smiles

So powerful was the response to Sarah Palin, and Joe the Plumber, and Tito the builder (with whom I hung in the Fox News Channel DC green room one morning while we were both waiting to go on just before the election), that the domestic insurgency was so frightened that they went to extraordinary lengths to vilify and discredit all of the above. They have also come after this author, albeit at a lower intensity.

They still fear and thus attack Palin with an irrational shrillness that betrays them.

In July 2009, in announcing that she would step down as Governor of Alaska before her term ended, Sarah Palin showed again why she resonates with so many Americans who cherish American values of duty, honor, service, tolerance, sense of justice and courage… and why she makes the left wing just plain nuts.

Sarah Palin is the anti-politician politician who, much to the consternation of the political and media elite, is a normal American who took it as a given that she had a duty to serve her family and community to the best of her abilities and in times that threaten to bring any one of us to our knees.

Her sense of public duty took the form of everything from car-pooling the hockey kids to becoming a community and political figure in a tiny Alaska town and finally in the governor's chair.

She stepped up to the plate to support her all too human family when reality intruded on our fantasy ideal family.

Palin and her family have survived the most critical gauntlet of them all… the mire of small town politics amplified by the spotlight of world attention. Having been so vetted she and her family were immune to the slings of the 'professionals' who grow increasingly irritated with what is to them an inexplicable bond that normal people feel with Mrs. Palin.

Faced with a growing, political, and malicious smear campaign against her, at great monetary cost to the state's taxpayers as much as to her, and even greater emotional cost on her family, she put family and community first.

To the shock of everyone (the "professionals") who expected her to follow their planned route to political slaughter, she took control of the table in one fell swoop. Like Minutemen picking off Red Coats in the New England woods, she just blazed a path through the wilderness around them and now she gets to make the rules with speaking, writing, activism, and perhaps even higher office.

By dropping this bomb in the middle of the first day of a four-day Independence Day Holiday, the story should have been dead on arrival in terms of running the news cycle. From all accounts it was Sarah and Sarah alone who decided to follow her gut and make her move when she did. I thought that there was a whopper of a Sarah did something story in the wings!

Not only was I wrong but also rather than disappear in the news hers became the only hard news story in a light news weekend. And her well-chosen words and emotions got the full attention of the media who suddenly trumpeted into action.

The brilliance of her timing though is in that the people who have really been caught off guard and unready are those in opposition to her, the ones who have been running the smear, you know - the Domestic Insurgency of the Left who tremble in fear. That includes no shortage of media spinmeisters who attend the Capitol Hill cocktail parties.

Since then Governor Palin has become a touchstone to ordinary people and unwashed masses. Those would be the Americans who Senate Majority Leader Harry Reid (D-Nevada) famously said that he could "smell" when then make their way to Washington as tourists.

While the occupiers party, the occupied have an emerging champion. A champion who plays for keeps it appears. I am glad that I am on her side.

Barack Hussein Obama Junior: A Clear and Present Danger

President Obama is a dangerous man surrounded by equally dangerous people.

He is by no means as dim as George W. Bush. That is the problem. Mr. Bush was well intentioned but out of his depth and surrounded by resume building, self-interests; Mr. Obama is a calculating and dangerous man. To save America we need the GOP to again be the party of America's heritage.

We will have to be the ones to make that happen. Truth be told, the GOP leadership has been one of the most unwavering and resolute obstacles to party reformation this author has encountered in my efforts at the grass roots level. As we saw during the '08 election campaign, the Republicans were like a boxer punching himself in the head repeatedly. To paraphrase a great black man, Muhammad Ali, all Obama had to do was *"dance like a butterfly"*... the GOP took care of the *"sting like a bee"* part all by itself.

So here is my advice, unsolicited, for the Republican Party (applicable to our entire government). Fire, banish, and send to Gitmo every single party operative who has lived inside the Beltway or been in charge of anything official for more than 30-seconds. Banish to some island every professional handler who tried to turn Sarah Palin from an All American realization of true equality and feminism into a bubble headed lightweight bimbo.

Ditto for the insulated fools, who were advising John McCain into the ground, and thank God that they are not air traffic controllers. Hey, they're not, are they? Okay, whew.

Our coup has to be an alignment of Americans who hold dear the foundational principles of this nation – the very Republican Principles that wrested the keys to Obama's peoples' chains from the Democrat Party of Jefferson Davis. The very Republican Principles that reward work and initiative, while granting help and charity to those less fortunate, must regain currency as well as reward for excelling. The Republican Principles that created a nation so great that to actually put its actions where its parchment words are now, risks annihilation at the hands of an enemy not just at the gate but also on the throne.

We are the ones who should and must *"do something"* and that is not *"pathetic"* (as termed by the Dead's Garcia). That is our sacred obligation and long past time when we reaffirm the immortal closing words penned by Thomas Jefferson in the Declaration of Independence:

> *"And for the support of this declaration, with a firm reliance on the protection of Divine Providence, we mutually pledge to each other our lives, our fortunes and our sacred honor."*

It is with that spirit that we have to take it upon ourselves to lobby for common sense and values and then translate that into results by working to elect, at the polls, those true inheritors of the legacy entrusted to us by the Founders.

Obama and his anti American orgy must be defeated.

Our nation has faced perilous times before but never in our brief history has our national survival been so gravely at risk. America is being challenged on all fronts. Men and societies thirsting for power are viciously attacking our economic, military, cultural, and political supremacy, and our country deserves better.

Chillingly though, for the first time since Tories were billeted among the citizenry of Boston our nation is occupied by a critical mass of the enemy. They fuel and feel off of useful idiots massed in numbers never seen before.

First they dumbed down the schools. Then an openly biased Mainstream Media misled us. Political Correctness has rewritten history, casting America as the villain… as it vilifies anyone with the courage to stand up and think.

The result is that, through no fault of our own, the next generation is the most politically illiterate, selfish, uneducated, historically and culturally illiterate voting public in the nation's history. That is not a commentary on that generation; it is just the sad result of policies that Obama vows to expand. Our country deserves better.

The stereotypical Welfare abuser, pumping out litters to snag a pay raise from working stiffs to keep her Caddy gassed up has been joined by Wall Street executives, bankers and investment houses all lining up at the trough for their piece of you and me. Big money and powerful people are lined up against the interests of America and her people, and our country deserves better.

The hopes of the entire Human Race deserve better than Barry Soetoro aka Barack Hussein Obama Junior.

In Chicago democrat politics the word "democrat" is spelled "mob" and Obama is living up to his heritage. Having learned from Al Gore's mistakes in attempting to steal the presidency via judicial fiat in 2000, Obama and the sinister forces behind him are worked hard to rig the 2008 election in their favor, nearly as hard as the Republicans worked through the administrations of George HW Bush, William Jefferson Clinton and (especially) George W Bush worked toward the same ends.

His cronies at ACORN are so neck deep in allegations of massive voter fraud and other crimes that they are disbanding and reconstituting under a variety of new names state by state. In Missouri, his 2008 campaign tried to coerce the state attorney general into prosecuting anyone who revealed any of the truths about Obama that contradict his "autobiography." Both the governor and attorney general of that state called him out on that and denounced the idea.

Obama was endorsed by a number of Islamic Terrorists and he is now paying them back, having reclassified Islamic Terrorism as a garden-variety crime to be handled by the same fine judges who routinely spring our own homegrown animals from stir to prey upon us and our children.

Our country deserves better than a president who calls "friend" a man who twice bombed a memorial to fallen cops in Chicago, and participated in planting of bombs at the United States Capitol Building and at the Pentagon. The friend's girlfriend and roommate were killed when an Improvised Explosive Device they were building exploded prematurely. That I.E.D. was being built to maim and kill innocent civilians.

The entire Human Race deserves a beacon of hope that does not hide in its glare the label of "stupid" for a policeman who enforces the law and a Mulligan for a Muslim who enters the Hellfire of Allah's kingdom at the cost of American lives.

All oppressed people, everywhere – even Muslims victimized by their own accident of birth pray to God that when they are in trouble and troops are on the horizon that the flag they march under is the Stars and Stripes.

Obama would remove even that faint glimmer of hope from the grasp of the hopeless.

But what does Obama's mentor Bill Ayers say about his past today? He told the New York Times that he does not regret being not just a terrorist bomber, but also one of their leaders. HE says that he – quote: "didn't do enough."!!! In fact, when asked if he would do it again said – and I quote Ayers again; "I don't discount the possibility."

Can his apprentice be far off of that page?

An American embodies the spirit of "Ask not what your country can do for you, ask what you can do for your country." Barack Hussein Obama Junior instead tells you what your country will do TO you, and FOR our enemies.

The American worldview is one where America stands strong and that Lady Liberty's torch forever remains a beacon of hope.

Barack Obama's worldview is that of the shadows he really represents, it is offensive to all who have any love of country or respect for individual rights.

Domestic Insurgents

We now know that Obama tried to convince the Iraqi government that they should discourage any withdrawal or drawdown of American troops in that country until after the election. That is not a surprise, as I have told you repeatedly; Obama and the Democrat Insurgency here are bathed in the blood of our own troops and untold numbers of innocent Iraqis. Obama and his people have fought both home and abroad to undermine our national security and the underpinnings of our world dominance.

The United States of America is the greatest nation to ever grace the face of this Earth. At no time in Human History has a society ever been founded upon the principles of freedom, responsibility, self-reliance and moral right… and then proceeded to literally tear itself apart trying to reach that ideal. We are the only ones to ever try and Obama now wants to extinguish the lights of the Shining City on the Hill.

That is why the Tea Party movement and all its constituent parts are important. He and the enemy ideology, embraced by the likes of House Speaker Nancy Pelosi and Senate Democrat Leader Harry Reid, and their flying monkeys must be stopped. Too many people died to leave us this grand legacy we call our country for us to hand it over the enemy.

Our nation IS at war. It is a war for the survival of a single flame, the flame of Liberty. This war is being fought not just in the deserts of the Middle East with guns but right here at home with lies. The biggest lie of all is becoming more and more apparent seemingly by the hour, and the Tea is reaching the boiling point.

The truth is that Obama & Co. represents a clear and present danger to our nation and your nation needs you to stand by her more than she ever has before. Our country deserves better, she has cradled and protected us; it is time to return the favor.

Barack Obama, our bad and why

"To understand the disease is to know the cure."

The author

We were warned about the coming of President Barack Hussein Obama Jr. and the accompanying overthrow of our Constitutional form of government. Oh, not Obama by name (at least until he became a viable candidate) and not just by me and the other Cassandras of talk radio and cable news channels for years before we ever heard his name, but by our Founding Fathers who recognized that as citizens' attention wanes, tyrants and despots will align themselves with fools to seize power. As Samuel Adams wrote to fellow Patriot James Warren on November 4, 1775:

"No people will tamely surrender their Liberties, nor can any be easily subdued, when knowledge is diffused and Virtue is preserved. On the Contrary, when People are universally ignorant, and debauched in their Manners, they will sink under their own weight without the Aid of foreign Invaders."

Thomas Jefferson, author of both the Declaration of Independence and the Bill of Rights even signaled a warning, ill heeded by the future, about the role Mainstream Media would play in pacifying the people with Bread and Circuses over critical information:

"The man who reads nothing at all is better educated than the man who reads nothing but newspapers."

It may be reasonably argued that the expense and availability of reading material and information (especially timely information) in the 18th Century was a daunting obstacle standing between a citizen and enlightenment, particularly when citizens of the day were pretty much pre-occupied with survival.

Yet there was no shortage of men (and women both heralded and unheralded) who managed to do just that; keep their families and their minds fed. To not be able to accomplish the same in this day and age, where we walk around in a literal "cloud" of instantly accessible critical information carries the concept of "lazy" to entirely new heights. In fact, if people worked nearly as hard at being informed and thinking for themselves as they do to avoid both; we would be a society right out of Plato's Atlantis.

Nonetheless, Mr. Jefferson could think of no safer repository for power than individual people despite the dangers. Of that he wrote:

> *"I know no safe depository of the ultimate powers of the society but the people themselves, (A)nd if we think them not enlightened enough to exercise their control with a wholesome discretion, the remedy is not to take it from them, but to inform their discretion by education. This is the true corrective of abuses of constitutional power."*

That is one of my favorite Jefferson quotes and one that the hard-core American Left despises. The entire point of the Democrat Party and affiliated and/or aligned kindred spirits of tyranny is to usurp your and my Creator granted rights to self-determination by any means necessary.

In the case of Barack Hussein Obama Jr. that means taking the accumulated abuses of Constitutional Power from the New Deal forward and putting them into a horrific display right in our national front window. It is then you, the citizenry, held to account and blame for those abuses. To the domestic insurgents and enemies currently in power, the obvious answer is to strip you of your rights since you caused the problem in the first place.

Problem is, as with so many other issues latched onto for distortion and power grabbing by these people there is a grain of truth in their point. But also as with so many of their other "solutions" the answer they offer up to "fix" it is the exact opposite of what should and must be done.

Think of the so-called Stimulus.

Eating our seed corn

All parties agree the problem arises from spending more wealth on non-productive wants than we have, at the expense of urgent needs that as a result go wanting.

The obvious solution to anything with a brain stem is to cut the unnecessary "wants" and go with the "needs." However, if your goal is to undermine America and destroy individual freedoms the answer is to spend even more, redefine wants as needs, and add a pile of both.

At home the analogy would be that you are broke, the kids are hungry and the repo man is at door yet your solution is to hit Disneyland for a few days and max a credit card or three.

But wait! Do we not need government to create jobs for us?

The obvious answer is no, simply because the government cannot create anything. It can only take, transform, slice a hunk off the top for themselves, and redistribute what is left. A job created by the government is not a job at all, it is simply a different kind of dependency designed to placate the vocal and project an image of action.

For example, the gentlemen on the next page...

Welcome to government work.

These fellows are part of a crew of Iraqis "hired" by the US Military to move a big pile of sand from where they had been paid to put it to another spot, mere feet away. When finished with that task, their next task was to move it back again.

I took this picture in July 2005, in a raging sand storm that had us trapped on the ground at the airport, where these men had been assigned.

That is a job created by government and is the only kind of job government can create. Government can only create that kind of make-work job by confiscating resources from the actual job creation machinery (you, me and the rest of the private sector) and in the process actually destroying not only existing jobs, but aborting new ones before they can be even envisioned, let alone happen.

Government bailouts and make-work jobs distort and pervert the economic system and created dead end tasks in return for what is basically a charity hand out, not for the purposes of actually helping but rather to create a dependency. That dependency translates into another foot soldier in the cause of government in perpetual growth mode, which requires an also perpetual mugging of the productive members of society.

Farmers have a saying about the sacrifice of the long term for the sake of a fleeting short term during a bad crop season. "Don't eat your seed corn" is a warning that while you may be hungry today but you will starve to death tomorrow if you fill your belly now with those kernels of corn seed that you must have in order to grow new crops next season. If you do eat your seed corn you will be less hungry for the moment but you will also be left with no seeds with which to grow any subsequent meals.

America's seed corn is the incentive provided by reward for effort and innovation. The field in which these sees are planted and from which great prosperity and advances for the entire human race have sprung is our capitalist economic system. From that rich crop we fund all of our societal needs as well as clear fresh ground for more planting, which in turn produces more prosperity.

Starting with Franklin Roosevelt's New Deal socialism we began munching on our seeds right up until now, when our seed bin is rapidly being consumed and is infested with parasites and maggots of all descriptions.

How can something like that happen? Simple. We let it.

The seed (sorry, pun irresistible) of truth that we are face with here has been repeated countless times at Tea Party Express events by many of our speakers, Joe "the

Plumber" Wurzelbacher included. Nearly his entire presentation to Tea Partiers (and anybody who will listen) is to admonish citizens for failing to fulfill the true obligation of citizenship.

That obligation and accompanying duty were perhaps not first but certainly best by Founding Father Thomas Paine who said:

> *"Those who expect to reap the blessings of freedom, must, like men, undergo the fatigue of supporting it...It is the duty of the patriot to protect his country from its government."*

The domestic enemies of this nation have systematically dismantled the world's premiere educational system and set about engaging social policies designed to prey upon and destroy cherished and critical American institutions such as; community, church, families, initiative, ambition and even dreams of a better life.

They have carefully nurtured and reinforced a mass culture of non-involvement and sold the most vulnerable among us into a culture of dependency. Hand in hand with that is a culture of greed facilitated to neutralize any significant opposition.

Bail outs for example. The introduction of the cousin ideologies of fascism and socialism have led to an America where today the state either owns or tightly controls the means of production, which means the state controls the creation and destruction of wealth both national and personal.

The rich and powerful are exempt from the consequences of their foolishness, failures, and crimes just as the working stiff on the assembly line if forced by this new economic order to bear the full cost. That cost is imposed in any number of ways ranging from stunted pay and benefits (if not total loss of self-sufficiency). The beneficiaries of this new economic order reward the politicians by keeping them in power and perpetuating the system that takes from the masses and enriches the few.

Doubt me? Which government programs are being threatened with cuts or elimination? Welfare, Social Security, Medicare, parks, police, fire.... essential services some constitutionally allowed, some a part of the fabric of our system simply because they are there and heretofore have (in the minds of some) served a needed role.

Do the bailouts and bonuses face cuts? Projects like the late Congressman John Murtha's' (D-PA) now infamous international airport to nowhere?

No, when times get tough in a system the likes of which we are being herded into it is the rulers who are not only protected but also indeed enriched. You and I, well we get to eat cake.

Enter Obama

In 2008 a people stripped of their virtue and saddled with the above turned to an invader both internal *and* external.

I am not even making reference to the open secret that Mr. Obama is improbably a native-born citizen of the United States.

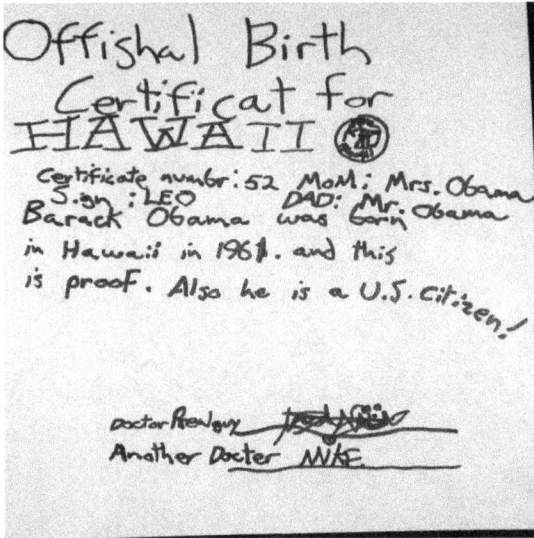

Even lacking the questions surrounding his citizenship, Mr. Obama would still be the carrier of an external invader. This invader is a brutal monster that dominates the world, and if not for the United States who have continued though history unchallenged.

That invader is an idea.

The idea is one perpetuated by and for the elite, for the party apparatus. It is an idea that feeds on the notion that all men are created equal, provided they are of a protected class. They are the professional politicians and functionaries who make and apply the law. They are the people who sit at the top of corporate food chains and manipulate the political class. They are people who together make the rules and can (and do) change them on a whim to suit their ends.

Mind you, there is no central control room where all of this is being orchestrated. What "they" are is people who have come to depend on the system for all that they have.

What they have ranges from private jets, access, and privilege to welfare checks and public housing. They all have something to lose when confronted with another powerful idea. That idea is called "America" and it is an idea that empowers the individual and by its very nature erases artificial advantages.

America is liberty, the opportunity for happiness and prosperity, the ability to leave a legacy for the future.

We Americans may be fat and lazy beneficiaries of that idea but woe be to the tyrant in training who seeks to snatch that idea from our grasp.

Liberals

"We are in an ideological war between the principles of Jefferson and Madison and those of Marx and Lenin."

The author on the Tea Party Express

"The English follow the principle that when one lies, one should lie big, and stick to it. They keep up their lies, even at the risk of looking ridiculous."

- Joseph Goebbels,

From Churchill's "Lie Factory" published in *Die Zeit ohne Beispiel* (Munich: Zentralverlag der NSDAP., 1941), pp. 364-369.

"Never give a sucker an even break."

W.C. Fields, from the film of the same name,
Hollywood USA, 1941

'" Political correctness is a societal HIV and America has a full blown case of AIDS."

The Author

C oming of age in the 1970's was difficult enough. My generation, at the tail end of the baby boom, was the first to venture into a world lacking clear moral standards of right versus wrong or a learned sense of duty or obligation. The Greatest Generation, the one that dispatched the Axis Powers, freed Europe, and produced John F. Kennedy, also unfortunately produced the generation that began our march down the path in the exact opposite direction in which the slain president had sought in his inauguration speech. *"Ask not what your country can do for you; ask what you can do for your country"* became *"grab for what you can get and run because you're entitled."* Those poor souls of Gen X and beyond, who had the misfortune to be raised in this world by the products of the 1960's "Me Generation" or those that followed slipped into a Culture of Dependency that threatens to consume our national heritage and the future hopes of Mankind.

Hand in hand, with the collapse of the spirit of JFK's words, came the removal from public life the *"Creator,"* acknowledged by our founders as the wellspring of our blessings and of all human rights.

The creator was replaced by an ever-shifting base of situational ethics which measures the morality of an act against the relative perceived morality (or lack thereof) of the party we would have previously labeled *"victim."* This measure incorporates a moral superiority automatically conferred upon the party we would have previously labeled the *"offender."* This reversal of normal roles arises in the mind of a liberal from the bizarre notion that society causes the criminal actions of individuals. That belief in effect lays the blame for crime on the victim and exonerates the criminal because the victim (as a part of society from which the criminal is inexplicable excused by the liberal mind) caused the criminal to behave as he did.

Argue with a liberal, see that they *are* mentally ill...

The author (right) attempting to communicate with a San Francisco liberal. Photo credit: Holly Williams

Dr. Lyle H. Rossiter Jr. is a forensic psychiatrist of some thirty-five years experience. In his 2006 book, *The Liberal Mind: The Psychological Causes of Political Madness* [1] Rossiter provides results and conclusions from his extensive research and experience dealing with dysfunctional minds. He has been a guest on my own radio program and makes a very convincing case for Savage's opinion.

Rossiter addressed on my radio program what he calls *"the psychopathology of the Liberal Mind"* and attributes liberalism to a deep-seated need to control, arising from childhood issues. Notice that he uses the word *"tyrant"* interchangeably with *"liberal"* in the excerpt on that very issue (retrieved from his web site rather than my show so as to be free from any bias of mine):

> *"Rather, the adult drive toward omnipotent control of others, in any arena whatever, is rooted in fears of separation, abandonment, loss or abuse--the residual effects of early attachment gone wrong. The need to dominate others arises from the tyrant's need for absolute assurance that the catastrophic loss of dependency or the pain of abuse so devastating to him in his earliest years will not be repeated. In his determination to control the world, he constantly defends himself against what Karen Horney aptly described as the most basic of human fears: being alone and helpless in a dangerous, indifferent world, the nightmare of the abandoned, terrified child. Persons plagued with such fears easily conclude that it is in their greatest interest to dominate others, or to imagine that they can, and to set about achieving that goal through the manipulation of government power."* [2]

This primal fear of abandonment and need to control leads liberals to the hypothesis of collective guilt absent individual accountability and is the cornerstone of hard-core, left wing thought.

Collective guilt = individual immunity

Liberal dogma holds that rights are license. This license is granted not by a Creator but by the liberal and remains your "right" so long as you exercise that "right" in accordance to the wishes and whims of the prevailing Groupthink. Do not ever expect to encounter a liberal using their own logic of license to defend your gun rights or your town's local nativity scene this Christmas for example. That is because to exercise either Right at all is counter to the Obama-Reid-Pelosi & company belief that you haven't such rights at all.

Things like consequences and responsibility don't exist, so long as the conditions of the license granted are observed. Stray from that path or dare to exercise your "right" as if it were nullify your immunity. In traditional systems admired by the Left, that can mean punishment up to and including death. If you have any doubt just grab yourself an Ojai Board and ask the ghosts of Stalin or the victims of the Cultural Revolution in Red China.

Dr. Rossiter again on what he calls "The Madness of Modern Liberalism":

"What the liberal mind is passionate about is a world filled with pity, sorrow, neediness, misfortune, poverty, suspicion, mistrust, anger, exploitation, discrimination, victimization, alienation and injustice. Those who occupy this world are

"workers," "minorities," "the little guy," "women," and the "unemployed." They are poor, weak, sick, wronged, cheated, oppressed, disenfranchised, exploited, and victimized. They bear no responsibility for their problems. None of their agonies are attributable to faults or failings of their own: not to poor choices, bad habits, faulty judgment, wishful thinking, lack of ambition, low frustration tolerance, mental illness or defects in character. None of the victims' plight is caused by failure to plan for the future or learn from experience. Instead, the "root causes" of all this pain lie in faulty social conditions: poverty, disease, war, ignorance, unemployment, racial prejudice, ethnic and gender discrimination, modern technology, capitalism, globalization and imperialism. In the radical liberal mind, this suffering is inflicted on the innocent by various predators and persecutors: "Big Business," "Big Corporations," "greedy capitalists," U.S. Imperialists," "the oppressors," "the rich," "the wealthy," "the powerful" and "the selfish." [3]

Excluding the degree to which our lives are controlled or not controlled by that which we can't yet understand, we are the master of our own fates on this Earth. We make the beds in which we must sleep and all of the accoutrements; like government, laws, rights, freedoms and more – even organized religion are simply tools and avenues created in order that we may take that control and realize our full potential; economically, socially, spiritually, culturally and otherwise.

Either you can use these tools to take control and excel, or you can be a dishonest liberal and use them as weapons to oppress and suppress those who attempt to excel, thus satiating your frightened inner child without having to break a sweat.

In that respect, being a liberal is not all that different from being a union thug. If you belong to a union and even attempt to put in an extra few minutes to finish a job, your union representative will quickly threaten that you will be facing disciplinary action. Liberals put this principle to work in society by penalizing those who succeed or even try, and rewarding those who fail to even.

Conservatives are not immune to that wrong-headed perspective. For example, Second Amendment purists who fail to recognize that the Constitution is a balancing act and that each and every right enumerated and implied also carries limitations. All rights carry varying degrees of responsibility and consequences, even in the event of their proper and legal use.

That kind of blind spot is only human because it is in our nature to see the world as revolving around us, individually. We all do it. The difference is that liberals truly believe that they are the center of the universe because their perspective is one of the wounded, petulant child, so well explained by Dr. Rossiter.

---

[1] *"THE LIBERAL MIND: The Psychological Causes of Political Madness"* By Lyle H. Rossiter, Jr., M.D. USA 2006

[2] "Liberty Mind.com" Lyle H. Rossiter, Jr. MD. USA

[3] ibid

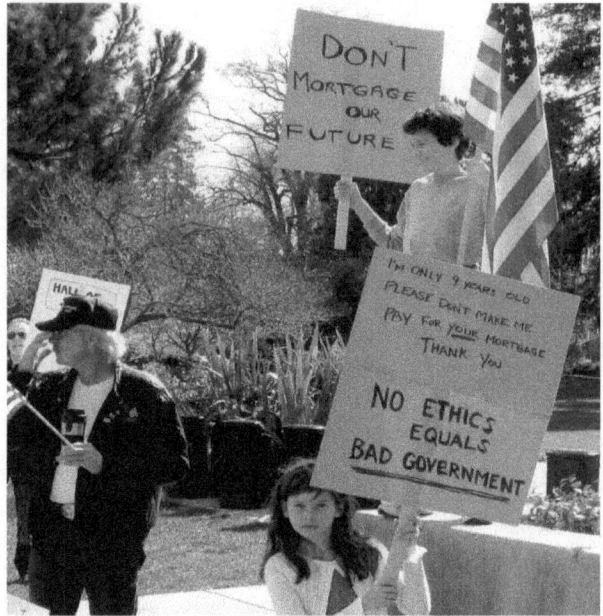

How this liberal child grew up to be an American adult

L ike many kids of my generation, I was raised largely by a 21" Zenith black & white TV. The fictional skills and social cues that I learned from watching shows like *McHale's Navy*, *F-Troop*, and *Hogan's Heroes*, became the real world coping skills that helped me negotiate a public school system designed to train factory workers for menial jobs. If not for *Captain Kangaroo's* constant admonition to always, say *"please and thank you,"* I might not have any normal social skills at all.

Later the schools switched from education to esteem issues and courses such as *"Superman as literature"* replaced English classes. *"Futurism"* and *"Science Fiction"* replaced

---

more English courses (I still have my report card and school handbook showing these!). Classroom debates over Vietnam raged (with the teachers making the expected anti-war speeches) and replaced the Pledge of Allegiance.

At some point, learning became forbidden too. I have vivid memories of being punished for reading too far ahead of even the advanced kids. The system was that we were given an assignment to do and were to never go beyond that, in order that the entire class stay together. I was testing at a nearly college level for reading and comprehension in grade school, in a public school system where mediocrity was the standard.

In that environment, it was critical to prevent kids like me from advancing. That was because before even my first day in school, it had been determined by the school that I would be blue collar tracked as factory fodder. So, the TV scripts became my survival strategy in a social system where excelling was prohibited to my caste.

My parents both worked, both came from families that could have re-written the definition of "dysfunctional" had such a word even existed at the time. There was no such word and everyone around us was the same way, heck the whole miserable and rotting mill town outside of Boston was the same. We knew no different. Social institutions were not in the picture. Even the local youth recreation programs were where you went to get beaten up, so they were places to be avoided.

Church was a toss up. My mother is Catholic and my father a Congregationalist Protestant (the church I was baptized in but left a long, long time ago.) Most of my friends were either devout catholic or secular protestant.

One thing I figured out early on was that none of that seemed the least bit relevant. The only church I ever saw as a source of social justice or even Earthly effort was the AME Zion church on my street. With an all black congregation and ministered by a black African missionary and he, and his church were on the front lines of the Civil Rights Movement

I lived at 13 Leroy Street in Attleboro, Massachusetts; the church was at 30 Leroy Street. The street was named "Leroy" because it was once farmland owned by an abolitionist. His barn was part of the Underground Railroad and after the Civil War it was an area where former slaves began their new lives. *"Leroy"* was not a complimentary name for the street and our neighbors where all blue collar, working poor Anglo (like us), recently arrived Portuguese, some blacks, and the church. Ironically enough, probably the most prosperous family on the street was a black family that owned a flower shop in nearby Providence, Rhode Island.

The little black church was also my very first experience with the sheer terror of being a clear minority in my mostly white (albeit wrong side of the tracks) neighborhood. I couldn't have been more than 6 or 7 years old when I decided to attend a service there one Sunday, because it seemed far more worth the time than either the boring and milquetoast Congregationalist services or the incomprehensible Roman Catholic services to which I was accustomed.

I was the only white face in a sea of what seemed to be millions of black people. I know now that the room seats maybe 200 people, but at the time, I had never seen so many black people in one place ever. I was terrified. I had no idea that there were that many black people in the world!

The reverend knew me from the neighborhood and he and his congregation welcomed me and were as pleasant as they were curious, but, in the end, I chickened out and took the first opportunity to make for the exit.

I was lucky though. Growing up outside of Boston meant that I could not avoid being inundated with political and social debate (not to mention racial and ethnic diversity). Talk radio stations were burning up the airwaves with exciting and provocative dialogue about war and race and other fiery issues, sometimes at a loud volume and accompanied by talk hosts leading listeners into the streets.

A healthy and feisty newspaper market offered several major dailies, each with a different editorial slant. My ace in the hole was family in Orange County, California. The OC was my Mecca and it did not take long for me to incorporate The Orange County Register, then far a more conservative newspaper than now, and legendary (now late) conservative Anaheim TV showman Wally George into my diet of the Boston Globe, the Boston Herald -Traveler and the Boston Record American and news periodicals.

I listened, read, and watched tumultuous events in American History play out, often on the same cobblestones where the nation was conceived and fought for birth. I simply cannot overstate the sense and reverence of history

that engulfs one while agitating for Right, on the very spot where the Boston Massacre happened, or on the streets around the Old North Church of Paul Revere fame. Nor can I overstate the value of having all of this coming to me through vastly different filtered lenses in an era where the mass media was as varied and nuanced as the rest of society, a blessing not afforded us today.

Nevertheless, we were by then a society that had begun to abandon the institutions and systems which anchored its moral moorings in favor of situational ethics. Just the same, enough of the old ideas remained and my parents ingrained some basic concepts of responsibility and of right and wrong, but they had to do so without benefit of the community and social fabric that had guided previous generations. At the same time, Dr. Spock's musings were turning my entire generation into an uncontrolled, social experiment, which amounted to 'if it feels good, do it' and taught parents that clear standards of right and wrong were, in fact, always wrong.

Molding children had fallen out of favor at the dawn of the age of Political Correctness. The catastrophic new standard was to allow children to "find themselves" and started the march toward creating a population of feral children. Thus, America began her descent into a PC age in which to determine the morality of an act has now become decried as judgmental, intolerant, or – here is the big liberal nuke; racist.

I, like many of you, had to take the shards of those ideas and figure out how to somehow assemble them into a functional worldview, and that is something for which you definitely do not want to borrow from TV shows that now live late night on basic cable, especially without benefit of the good Captain Kangaroo for balance.

To overcome that, it took both directed and self-learning, much contemplation, and experimentation with ideas, spiritual searching, travel, and some 30 years of arguing with people on the radio.

The good news is that the tide has turned and it's not so much "argue" any more.

The Tea Party Movement is a perfect storm that has swept aside any inclination for one to feel ashamed or somehow cowed to hold and openly express pride for nation, ethics, and Constitutional Rights for all. It has done so in the blink of an historical eye and completely changed the game.

Until the Tea Parties to proclaim love for country was to invite scorn or ridicule and to be reviled by the domestic enemy.

Well, hey, we're getting' there. Think salmon going upstream. They've got dams on their main streams working against them and we have the damn mainstream media working against us.

The Tea Part Express and your influence dominated the CPAC (Conservative Political Action Conference) 2010 event, the largest and most influential Constitutional Conservative event in the nation. 9/12 Founder and Fox News' Glenn Beck was the keynote speaker for the event that had one of the highest attendances on record... 10,000 people in a hotel/conference center with a capacity for 7,000 people.

The sting of the oft hurled epithet "RACIST!" is gone, fear of disapproval or being labeled GASP!) "right wing" has dissipated as the sheer number of people identifying themselves with the Tea Party Movement has rocketed to more than 60-million in just one year.

This is a true grassroots, American Citizen driven groundswell of ordinary men and women. Little kids and old geezers alike, gun-toting NRA diehards arm in arm with Brady Law evangelists. Next to them a handful of uncompromising pro-lifers mingling with abortion rights activists, each individual celebrating and coming to the defense of the American Constitutional system of government that protects their rights to hold and defend that which the passionately believe.

God Bless them, for it is they – it is YOU – ALL *EQUAL*, in their/OUR diversity that the Creator intended us to be. That is something that no man, no tyrant, Mr. Obama included will ever wrest from our hands.

As Prometheus gave Man fire, the Founding Fathers gave Man a slice of Liberty and dared us to nurture and grow it, while warning us that it would be but a fleeting moment in history in the event we neglected our Divine Gift.

One year ago I was a pessimist. Today, after speaking at more than 120 Tea Parties in towns and cities across the nation I am invigorated by all this wonderful Tea!

SHOWDOWN IN SEARCHLIGHT

★ SATURDAY, MARCH 27, 2010 ★
★ HIGH NOON (12:00 PM) ★

Sponsored by www.TeaPartyExpress.org

Tea Parties, an American reinvigoration not a revolution

In 2006 and through the 2008 election, both the economy and Republicans were on the ropes and both mortally wounded. The Culture of Dependency reached a critical mass, as those who feed off those who provide, reached unheard of numbers, and those on the margins fell into desperation and were being swept up by the Siren Song of Wrong. Like the lost boys in Pinocchio, feasting on chocolate mountains and Gummy Bear raindrops in Never Land not realizing that they were slowly sprouting ears, tails and turning into asses, these poor desperate souls were seduced by the false magic elixir of the Culture of Dependency.

Thus began the first Great Depression of the 21st Century and the full implementation of the Socialist Agenda that underlies liberalism.

You can either gnash your teeth over the housing bubble burst and economic collapse and drink the elixir of Socialism, or you can realize that this is one of those rare times when you can buy today for a nickel the land upon which the new mall will be built tomorrow and act accordingly by seizing the opportunity.

Barack Hussein Obama and his "Army" were elected on a promise of tearing up Capitalism and prosperity and replacing it with the misery of Socialism… and they are delivering on their promises as no other political crowd has ever delivered!

Republicans, indeed patriotic Americans in general, need to make a fundamental change in how they view themselves and what happened November 7, 2006 and November 4, 2008. On those Election Days, the barking Moon Bats of the Democrat Party extremes wrested control of both houses of Congress, and then the White House from a GOP in disarray. It wasn't hard at all; the Republican Party had lost its way. It was as if the party had buried its principles nearly simultaneously with its greatest champion, and, by extension, America's champion, since Abraham Lincoln - Ronald Reagan.

What Republican candidates experienced in these past elections was political Darwinism, pure and simple. Evolution invariably results in both opportunity and danger. In this case, a burst of political evolutionary activity the weak, the stupid, many of the corrupt (or at least ethically challenged), the simply unlucky, and those who betrayed their base were sent to the political hereafter. Those strong or lucky enough to survive were sent scrambling to digest and understand and adapt to the new climate.

The message delivered these elections past was unquestionable in its volume and clarity. The People disavowed themselves of the political class that has abandoned all pretense of serving and is now in an unholy league with the domestic enemies of this country.

Probably nobody illustrates the utter corruption of the system better than California Governor Arnold Schwarzenegger. The action movie star is also a Kennedy family nephew by virtue of his marriage to Maria Schriver. In national television interview after national television interview, I am constantly asked how a republican could be elected governor in California. The answer is easy. We didn't elect a republican, we elected a liberal democrat – a Kennedy taboot – who ran as a republican because that party didn't have half-a-dozen wealthy celebrities lined up to claim the office from disgraced democrat governor Gray Davis.

The party embraced Schwarzenkennedy because the state GOP leadership was a group of contemptuous fools who were fat and happy in their niche and saw no reason to fully participate in the political process. The party leadership bought into the falsehood that Arnold's celebrity offered them a chance to get back into the game. The admission they paid on our behalf was state party's soul and the state's fiscal and perhaps even social solvency.

You may have discerned, from my previous statements about Governor Arnold Schwarzenkennedy, that even more disturbing to me than the lack of media attentiveness to the details of the Governator is the utter oblivion of the state republican party.

The morning after the November 7, 2006 mid-term near extermination of the California GOP, then party chairman, Duf Sundheim, put on a stunning display of how a person in a vegetative state would sound if ambulatory.

On the other hand, Terri Schivao probably had more situational awareness than Duf. I say that because even she, in a persistent coma, would have had a hard time being unconscious enough to come up with the gem of a quote that Duf gave to KCBS Radio (740 AM) in San Francisco, as he stood among the wreckage of his party the morning after it was driven into the sea. Duf (or, Dufus, as he was known on my radio program) told the interviewer that the election was an *"example"* of the *"benefits"* of a *"bipartisan"* approach and that California is going in the *"right"* (as in "correct") direction, Republican-wise.

A hard-core alcoholic couldn't do denial so well, even with the help of a prolonged personal visit from Mr. Jack Daniels on an excursion to Boone's Farm. Skid Row junkies are quicker to recognize their plight.

The general consequence of this kind of GOP stupidity and treachery was a massive rise in informed voters *tuning*-out (at the expense of *turning* out) and an algae boom in the shallow end of the gene pool at the polls. It has been said that those who show up run the world. That republicans were seeming to be intentionally working as hard as they could to discourage people from showing up is something your humble scribe began warning his radio, television, and print audiences long ago.

Oblivious to the obvious, the GOP leadership went AWOL on anything resembling principle or even appearing the slightest bit aware of the depth of the hole that they had dug. Indeed, George W. Bush wielded the most damaging shovel of all as he worked over time to cement his place in history as perhaps the worst and most unintentional damaging executive ever. Almost, as if by design, he seemingly cobbled himself together a composite of Herbert Hoover, Jimmy Carter, and Woodrow Wilson resulting in sheer incompetence on a broad range of issues.

The issues are simple enough to grasp and few in number. Among them: *"It's the economy stupid,"* to which *"Dubya"* and the brain trust around him answered with a massive transfer of your and my money. Our money became reward money for irresponsible corporate debt. Mr. Bush put homeowners and small business people in the position of having to pay not only their own bills, but also the bills run up by people to whom those citizens owed money.

Some of those big corporations triple dipped; getting bail out money taken from working stiffs like you, me and Joe the Plumber, plus the payments we owed them and many called it a Hat Trick with bankruptcy filings so that they could deadbeat on their legitimate corporate expenses and keep their booty. Outrageous bonuses and spa visits soon threatened to consume three-quarters of a trillion dollars of our money set aside to *"bail out"* the economy.

By Barack Hussein Obama's 100th Day in office that number was over $12-*Trillion.*

Sensible Americans know that paying taxes is pretty basic. It is how we fund the essential services and obligations of government... the operative word in that sentence being "essential." We ask the government to do its essential duties of protecting our individual rights at home and safeguard us abroad from marauding global corporate interests, and keep those interests and the government out of our families, homes, and personal lives. For that, we have been and are being vilified as *"unpatriotic"* (Joe Biden) and *"racist"* (Obama supporters).

Reasonable immigration policies receded into the background, as the crumbling US economy sent illegal aliens packing up to find greener grass on the southern side of the US border. Amazing gains and forward moves in rebuilding Iraq became overshadowed by lies – like Barack H. Obama's assertion that the US Military aims bombs at women and children.

Virtually every major Islamic Terror organization, and no shortage of individual nut cases on the planet, was in the news either endorsing, what I call the Domestic Insurgency represented by Nancy Pelosi (US House Speaker) and Harry Reid (US Senate Majority Leader) and their minions, or "congratulating" US voters for surrendering to Allah's divine will on election day 2006. The same crowd was more restrained on Election Day 2008 but already on record as endorsing and even working the phones for Obama, some even from terrorist occupied Gaza. [1].

The Democrat Party, now firmly in control of our government and under the control of its extremes, will implode. That is a given as surely as the WMD attack(s) that we all know are on the way, now that the extremes have stepped up to the prayer rung. They are determined to destroy this nation as we know it and whether or not they are successful depends on whether or not we can stop them. And stop them we will!.

Here, is where both opportunity exists and danger lurks because it is now a race to see who will emerge, and the choice is clear. It is between a newly energized, back to basics GOP, or President Obama and the absolute final chapter in America's all too brief stint as a world super power and custodian of human rights. There is no in-between and what happens is frighteningly enough up to the tattered, surviving remains of Lincoln's and Reagan's Grand Old Party and whether or not there are enough of us prepared to take the reigns and depose the party of its fools so that we may set the nation on a straight and true course once again.

---

[1] al Jazeera February 24, 2008 – reported at MarkTalk.com October 10, 2008 http://www.marktalk.com/blog/2008/10/10/working-hard-to-elect-obama-as-president-islamic-terrorists-in-gaza-form-gazans-for-obama-and-man-phone-bank-to-call-usa-voters-and-drum-up-support-for-obama-obama-holocaust-part-ii/

Liberalism, the 'real' racism

I do not presume to rewrite the words of Thomas Jefferson but when he wrote in the Declaration of Independence: *"...all men are created equal..."* it would have been helpful if he had added an asterisk directing the gentle reader to the implied fine print behind his thought. That would have saved us a good deal of time and trouble battling liberals who have twisted the great man's thought into one of a guaranteed equality for all, at all stages of life, and to be accomplished by penalizing and discouraging success while rewarding and protecting mediocrity and admiring utter lack of ambition as a desirable trait.

Very simply put, we are all born buck-naked and given by our Creator a basket full of rights – one of which is the right to use the rest wisely, foolishly or not at all. The Constitution enumerates many of those rights and implies many others but only as a matter of law. The Constitution gives us nothing; it exists as a handcuff to deter tyranny – as benevolent as liberals would have us believe it is possible for a tyrant to be anyhow.

What the Constitution is not is a guarantee that we remain equal forever. Neither does the Constitution provide relief for those actually born unequal. Physical and mental infirmities are the Deity's province not Mister Jefferson's. Our society and individuals within, make Herculean efforts to level that particular playing field, but the notion that a man with no legs is equal in all things to an Olympic athlete is absurd. Equally absurd is the idea that my non-existent math skills should make me a peer of Albert Einstein.

In today's wacky America, I should be enlisting the aid of the American Civil Liberties Union to file suit for both the legless guy and myself because clearly our "rights" to equality have been violated. Rather I choose to acknowledge that I never did my math homework because I have little aptitude for it, and the job of the school was to teach me how to overcome that and learn.

The school preferred to continue its course of preparing me to kick a foot-press in a jewelry factory and I chose to find a path away from that machine that did not involve math. No villains or lawsuits there. Things are what they are and that's just the name of that tune.

In 2006, the Boston University College Republicans joined a short list of college activists attempting to sail the treacherous shoals of pointing out the immorality of race-based scholarships. What was notable about this particular effort was that the group approached the University and its minority population "leaders" first.

The BUCP realized that their entire point would be lost if they simply floated their misnamed "Caucasian Achievement Award" because it would immediately become a target for charges of racism. So, they explained their position and convinced those minority "leaders" that they were sincere in their efforts to instigate constructive dialogue.

The reaction from the minority "leaders" was very interesting. They granted to the republican group the presupposition of sincerity and even agreement with the group's position!

Sara-Marie Pons, speaking as co-chairman of something called the Admissions Student Diversity Board at BU, admitted to The Daily Free Press (a BU student newspaper) that she agreed with the republicans that racial preferences (affirmative action) are *"contradictory to our American ideals of freedom and equality."* [1]

That is a stunning admission for a budding young professional in the racism propagation industry! You will never hear the good Reverend Jessie Jackson or big Al Sharpton ever concede such territory.

But wait, there's more.

Having recognized the wrong of racial preference, Ms. Pons went on to tell the paper that, despite the fact that such preferences are against everything this nation stands for, that *"American history justifies"* (emphasis is mine) continued racial preference programs! Then, as if that kneeling at the alter of evil isn't enough, Ms. Pons goes on to demonstrate an insulting (to minorities) plantation mentality by implying that minorities are too dim-witted to understand the value of an education and must be bribed, in order that their attention be attracted in that direction by saying: *"The scholarship* [race-based scholarships directed toward non-whites] *is there* (sic) *to increase the interest of students in that group to continue their education and reach the equality that we all strive for."* (Sic – and *sick* too) [2]

How many things can you spot wrong in that single sentence? They are multitude.

Let us start with the most obvious and that is the fallacy that somebody in that thought is striving for equality. Ms. Pons takes on the cloak of some 1930's black & white Tarzan movie great white bwana ready to flick her Zippo to the amazement of local natives concerned that a solar eclipse just ate the sun. I sputter at the very idea of this pious, self-righteous, racist woman anointing herself the moral, intellectual, and social superior to the dumb, godless savages who cannot be made to understand the importance of an education in the absence of a shiny object and maybe a handful of beads and seashells. The nerve of that woman!

Yet that attitude is the very foundation of affirmative action and racial preference. In a liberal's worldview, blacks and other minorities are likeable but clearly dim companion animals to be cared for and not to be asked anything of in return. While placid beasts, minorities to a liberal are chattel to be controlled and directed to the liberal's own end vision, which invariably is of that liberal being superior and "helping" the lower animals achieve their potential, which, is of course, hardly equal to the liberal's.

This thinking (if "thinking" is a word applicable to the likes of Ms. Pons) is a refined yet fundamentally unchanged racist view handed down through centuries, perhaps best represented in my personal library by the works of George Fitzhugh, a 19th century advocate for slavery.

Try this on for size. Remove the political correctness glasses that have been forcibly thrust upon you, take into account the context of the obsolete prose, and read below what Fitzhugh wrote in this excerpt from one of his commentaries published in 1857 and titled: The Universal Law of Slavery:

"He the Negro is but a grown up child, and must be governed as a child, not as a lunatic or criminal. The master occupies toward him the place of parent or guardian. We shall not dwell on this view, for no one will differ with us who thinks as we do of the negro's capacity, and we might argue till dooms-day in vain, with those who have a high opinion of the negro's moral and intellectual capacity.

Secondly. The negro is improvident; will not lay up in summer for the wants of winter; will not accumulate in youth for the exigencies of age. He would become an insufferable burden to society. Society has the right to prevent this, and can only do so by subjecting him to domestic slavery. In the last place, the negro race is inferior to the white race, and living in their midst, they would be far outstripped or outwitted in the chaos of free competition. Gradual but certain extermination would be their fate. We presume the maddest abolitionist does not think the negro's providence of habits and money-making capacity at all to compare to those of the whites. This defect of character would alone justify enslaving him, if he is to remain here. In Africa or the West Indies, he would become idolatrous, savage and cannibal, or be devoured by savages and cannibals. At the North he would freeze or starve.

We would remind those who deprecate and sympathize with negro slavery, that his slavery here relieves him from a far more cruel slavery in Africa, or from idolatry and cannibalism, and every brutal vice and crime that can disgrace humanity; and that it christianizes, protects, supports and civilizes him; that it governs him far better than free laborers at the North are governed. There, wife-murder has become a mere holiday pastime; and where so many wives are murdered, almost all must be brutally treated. Nay, more; men who kill their wives or treat them brutally, must be ready for all kinds of crime, and the calendar of crime at the North proves the inference to be correct. Negroes never kill their wives. If it be objected that legally they have no wives, then we reply, that in an experience of more than forty years, we never yet heard of a negro man killing a negro woman. Our negroes are not only better off as to physical comfort than free laborers, but their moral condition is better. The negro slaves of the South are the happiest, and, in some sense, the freest people in the world" [sic] [3]

Sound vaguely familiar? It should. It is exactly the point made by Dr. Lyle Rossiter (and elaborated upon in this book) about the self-perceived moral superiority of liberalism and its need to control those who occupy less worthy positions in the liberal belief system.

Would anyone care to show me how one of this county's best known late advocates of slavery in general and African slavery in particular, differs from the co-chairman of the Boston University Admissions Student

Diversity Board? The only difference I can detect is one of a refinement in the language used in the contemporary example in order to conceal the underlying point, which remains loathsomely identical to the inherently racist point made a century and a half ago without the modern obfuscation.

The bottom line is that one of the primary points of anything approaching American is that racism is wrong. That wrong is absolute and without qualification. Celebrating and sharing one's ethnic heritage and pride in that heritage is one thing, an enormously enriching and constructive thing.

In fact "Race" is a not even a biological term. Depending on the culture in which the concept is being used and/or the perspective of the observer "race" can mean anything about a person ranging from the natural; skin pigmentation and other visibly apparent inherited traits for example, to the arbitrary geographic or political origin such as: Asian or African, and now to the legal status of a person; i.e. you are a "racist" if you oppose illegal immigration because "immigrant" has now entered the scared list of human "races" which to offend is to become a pariah.

Culture is a different story. Humans live in a mind numbing variety of cultures. Not all cultures are equal. Those cultures that comprise these United States are without a doubt the richest and most diverse to ever assemble in one place on Earth in our Race's existence and are to be celebrated, not smothered in an oppressive blanket of political correctness.

Would New York be New York without the Puerto Rican Day Parade, or could Boston be Boston without a big Saint Patrick's Day blowout, Chicago without Polish Pride or San Diego minus its Spanish heritage? How about Miami with out Jewish and Cuban cultural influences? Or the African and French influences in the American South? All of which have managed to join with hundreds of others to create something far greater than the sum total of its parts.

Pride in America is Pride in *ALL* these cultures, and the people who brought them to the party.

Pride in one's lineage becomes wrong and destructive the instant that pride transforms into perceived superiority of one over the perceived inferiority of another. There is no good that can be considered a just ends to the evil means of racism, whether that racism arises from Night Rider of the Ku Klux Klan or from the mouth of a liberal.

I will defer to Dr. William "Bill" Cosby and columnist Stanley Crouch in their diagnosis and prescribed remedies (admonitions) available to black Americans in particular (which also happens to be solid advice to Americans in general) and direct the reader to their respective bodies of works for deeper thought from a right perspective. But for those unfamiliar with the works of the two men it boils down to stop whining, stop hiding behind the straw man of race, stop making excuses and take responsibility for your own life.

It is hard to argue with that, although many try. It just so happens that they have now been proven wrong in a resounding denouncement of racism, even at the risk of our very nation. For my illustration of just how simply wrong the "America is Racist" crowd is I simply point to the current President of the United States.

---

[1] *BU group offers white scholarship; Award meant to protest race-based scholarships, Boston University Daily Free Press, November 21, 2006 by Clarissa Bottesini, Boston, Massachusetts*

[2] Ibid

[3] *The Black American; A Documentary History*, Third Edition, by Leslie H. Fishel, Jr. and Benjamin Quarles, Scott, Foresman and Company, Illinois, 1976, 1970

[*] More on the diagnosis of "Liberalism" as a mental dysfunction may be found in "The Liberal Mind: The Psychological Causes of Political Madness" by Dr. Lyle H. Rossiter 2006 Free World Books LLC, St. Charles IL.

Why "Under God" is important

"And can the liberties of a nation be thought secure when we have removed their only firm basis, a conviction in the minds of the people that these liberties are the gift of God?"

Thomas Jefferson [1]

Michael A. Newdow is a brilliant and busy man. He is an itinerant emergency room physician, an attorney, and destructive to the core.

You know Newdow as the Sacramento, California atheist who has been battling to remove "Under God" from the Pledge of Allegiance and "In God We Trust" from our money for several years. Lesser known is that his entire adventure in First Amendment law was sparked and driven almost entirely by his apparent personal mission to control or destroy a former shack up girlfriend with which he fathered a child.

Newdow is a father only in the biological sense of the word and has devoted his life and whatever source of income he is able to tap to hunting down and running the lives of his ex-girlfriend and daughter (nobody knows for sure where he gets his money; he shows a very low income but says that he has "savings" --- I'd lay you dollars to doughnuts that there is a liberal anti-God group out there funneling money in his general direction, but that is only my opinion). Newdow lives in Sacramento because that is where is east coast girlfriend fled with child to get away from him. [2]

The vermin that I consider the likes of Michael Newdow to be do serve one very important purpose though. They provide opportunity for us to revisit why those two words are in there and how they have become so important despite their dubious history.

The Pledge of Allegiance has its roots in the writing of turn of the century Baptist Minister Francis Belllamy. A Christian Socialist, Bellamy in 1892 took the Utopian ideas of an author cousin (Edward Bellamy) and composed a simple version of what we know as the Pledge of Allegiance for a Columbus Day celebration for a school in which he was not only the superintendent but also a representative on the committee of state superintendents of the National Education Association.

That is all well and good but apropos of nothing, for better or worse.

There were modifications over the decades but the operative words "Under God" were added by congress in 1954 following a lobbying campaign by the Knights of Columbus. Again, all fine and dandy but not to the point.

The point is that the unwitting collaboration of a socialist Baptist preacher, the Catholic Knights of Columbus, and the tweaking in-between arrived at an inadvertent yet inescapable truth. That truth is that America is impossible without God.

> *The Sacred Rights of mankind are not to be rummaged for among old parchments or musty records. They are written, as with a sunbeam, in the whole volume of human nature, by the Hand of the Divinity itself, and can never be erased or obscured by mortal power.*

> Alexander Hamilton [3]

No other society in the history of Mankind has ever attempted such a bold idea as that of universal human rights assigned as a course of nature, no different than the issuance of hair color, two arms, two legs, a head, eye color and those other aspects of our existence which we simply accept as being. The addition of something as intangible as human rights also assigned at birth by a Creator is not only unique to the United States but even in this day and age a huge pill to swallow for a world of gods as diverse as the humans who created them.

Think about that for a second. A collection of self-educated and phenomenally intelligent and inquisitive men sat down and made peace among all the competing versions of a Creator in which they were schooled. Granted, most of them shared similar views derived from their common Anglo – Christian backgrounds, yet they managed to create a religious agreement and accord for which there was no precedent and that the Human Race has since been unable to recreate.

The next few paragraphs may seem trivial or flip; I assure you that I am being neither. What I am doing in these next few paragraphs is arming you with information and ideas in language that even a liberal might be capable of understanding.

The idea of unalienable rights granted by a Creator is so elegant in its simplicity as to be blindingly obvious yet, to many, it sounds like either rocket science or some sort of religious statement. It is neither and the sheer beauty of the idea hinges on a simple concept; that is that what we wish not to muck up must be placed out of our reach. If we can't get to it then we can't break it.

Jefferson pioneered that very same notion of a Creator as a tool to create human rights but putting them out of reach of the humans. Not only do you use a version of this idea on your kids when you put the cookie jar away but contemporary twelve step programs use the very same idea. If you are in AA you know that you are told that it "doesn't make any difference if a doorknob is a god to you" so long as you have a higher power to lean on.

Okay, so the same plot line played out in the classic Disney feature "DUMBO." Dumbo never did need to clutch that feather to fly; he just needed to clutch something that he could believe in more than he believed in himself. Jefferson uses the Creator the same way friends of Bill at AA use his doorknob and a cartoon elephant uses a crow's feather.

No man can grant any right to another man, it is quite simply put: impossible. A man can only grant temporary privilege to another man. That which man grants man can, and usually does rescind. In order to be "unalienable" and thus a true "right," that right must be unassailable by any man. It must be granted from some place so far above man as to be unreachable. To risk another overly simplistic metaphor; to have true rights we must place them in a Creator's care for safekeeping on a shelf that we cannot reach.

In a supreme irony Michael Newdow's right to be an atheist and use that directionless belief to assault the foundation upon which that right stands is granted to Newdow by the very creator in which Newdow claims does not exist. Likewise, because the Creator blessed Newdow with rights and not man-made privileges, we are correctly helpless to force silence upon him or give him the treatment that he would get in an Islamic society for example.

Where America has lost its moral bearings on this issue and why Newdow is considered a big deal and not a petulant crank is in not enough of us understanding that the issue at hand has nothing to do with a pledge or patriotism. It is not some form of xenophobic grab to lay claim to the one and true God, nor is it religious in nature. If more Americans understood this issue then the likes of Michael Newdow would be powerless to hurt our nation. It is our own lack of understanding and faith in our nation, its founding principles and our own Creator, that empower the evil likes of the Newdows in the country.

Those two simple words: "Under God" make the Pledge of Allegiance a plain and unadorned acknowledgement that the United States of America is indeed the guardian of God-given unalienable rights and hence truly Ronald Reagan's vision of Mankind's Shining Light on the Hill [4].

[1] *"Notes on the State of Virginia"*, by Thomas Jefferson" 1782

[2] *"Under God" Iconoclast Looks to Next Targets*, by Evelyn Nieves, New York Times, July 1, 2002

[3] *"An essay, "The Farmer Refuted,"* by Alexander Hamilton 1775

[4] *"Farewell Address to the Nation"* by President Ronald Reagan, January 11, 1989, the Ronald Regan Library

Islam; a celebration of savagery

"We are at war. And our battle has only just begun. Our first victory will be one tract of land somewhere in the world that is under the complete rule of Islam. . . . Islam is moving across the earth. . . . Nothing can stop it from spreading in Europe and America."
Sheikh Abd al-Qadir as-Sufi ad-Darqawi [1]

W hy do the terrorists want to kill us? Who cares so long as we either deter or kill them first? If you really want to know just ask them, and that is as easy as going to your local library or logging on to Google because they've been nice enough to write it all down for you and have gone to great lengths to publish and distribute the answer.

I am not going to go into a painfully detailed 1,300+-year history of the 7th Century Death Cult we call "Islam" and how it came to be. Suffice to say that the story involves lots of bisexual men who are oddly homophobic and a psychotic pedophile, who coughed up this twisted and violent ideology during seizures in the desert, augmented by an inbred paranoia and an imposed ignorance acquired and reinforced over the centuries. The details of how my assailant came to be my assailant really do not concern me; I just want him contained or dead.

The modern day history of Islamic Jihad began when US President Jimmy Carter in 1979 dislodged a solid US ally, Muhammad Reza Shah Pahlavi – the Shah of Iran - from the Peacock Throne (theoretically an inherited crown of leadership in Persia, as Iran was known from the 6th Century until 1935) and allowed to be installed the Ayatollah Ruollah Khomeini. The elderly ayatollah was a leading proponent of violent jihad and immediately declared war on civilization with the taking of the American Embassy and hostages in Tehran. He also became the catalyst for a coalescing of the most violent extremes in a most backward and savage corner of the Earth.

Siding with his cronies and stooges (stooges like Jimmy Carter); he also set out to realize what his brand of the religion of peace considers its essence as explained by Sheikh Mortaza Motahari: *"Islam is the religion of agitation, revolution, blood, liberation, and martyrdom."* [2]. Khomeini also set about drawing his line in the sand with his New Year message of 1980 in which he claimed the mantel of revolutionary and leader of an all out *violent* jihad to *"Those who believe, fight in the Cause of Allah, and those who disbelieve, fight in the cause of at-taghut (Satan). So fight you against the allies of Satan; Indeed, the plot of Satan is weak."* [13] and to destroy existing political world order and western culture. The tool he chose was terrorism [3]. As it turns out, Islam was primed and ready to go.

> *"The world as it is today is how others have shaped it. . . . We have two choices: either to accept it with submission, which means letting Islam die, or to destroy it, so that we can construct the world as Islam requires."*
> Ayatollah Muhammad Baqir al-Sadr 1980 [4]

> *"Terror struck into the hearts of the enemies is not only a means, it is the end in itself....Once a condition of terror into the opponent's heart is obtained, hardly anything is left to be achieved. It is the point where the means and the end meet and merge....Terror is not only a means of imposing decision upon the enemy; it is the decision we wish to impose upon him".*
>
> Brigadier S.M. Malik, Pakistan [5]

In June of 1982, Khomeini, with the help of the Soviets, held the first international assembly of representatives from terrorist organizations and the states that support them in Tripoli, Libya. Emissaries from 240 terrorist and other vicious gangs, gathered along with ambassadors from 80 nations that support or sympathize with terrorism in order to find areas of ideological agreement that would allow for the coordination of their efforts. Libya, Iran, Syria, Cuba, and North Korea emerged as the "executive committee" of international terrorism. [6]

There is an intense politically correct claptrap surrounding these truths. It is one that denies to the terrorists' own face what the terrorists themselves repeat again and again and again and the mounting evidence that Islam is a dangerous and savage culture that must either be tamed to live among us or be excluded to the wild corners of the Earth.

The reaction of Americans to human tragedies anywhere, even in Moslem countries that hate us, is to embrace them and do whatever we can do to help. The reaction of Moslems to a human tragedy outside of their cult is dancing in the streets. Just like we all saw in the days following the 9/11 attacks when tens of thousands of followers of the religion of peace danced wildly in the narrow, filthy streets of their Third World hovels.

> *"Those Christians who kill in the name of their faith are acting contrary to the teachings of Jesus Christ; those Muslims who kill in the name of their faith are acting in accordance with the Qur'an."*

Dr. Ergun Caner (a former Muhajadeen, current Quranic and Bible scholar who abandoned Jihad for Christianity) to the author on the author's radio program

"Savage" is not an insult it is a description

Savage, —adjective

> 1. *fierce, ferocious, or cruel, untamed*
>
> 2. *uncivilized, barbarous, savage tribes*
> 7. *an uncivilized human being*

8. *a fierce, brutal or cruel person*
9. *a rude boorish person*

—*Synonyms* 1. wild, feral, fell; bloodthirsty. See CRUEL. 2. wild. 3. infuriated. 5. rough, uncultivated. 9. churl, oaf.

—*Antonyms* 1. mild. 2, 4. cultured. 5. cultivated. [7]

As you see above, "savage" is not even a judgmental term, it is descriptive. The word simply describes the level of civilization achieved by a given society, as measured against others, and usually from the point of view of the observer. To be fair to Islam that means that there is a built-in Western bias and a mostly Anglo–Judeo-Christian one at that. However, we are the Westerners in question and like it or not, by our standards, Islam is absolutely a savage culture that worships violent death both inflicted and suffered as the crowning achievement that will grant one eternal life – and 72 virgins.

Islam's societal and cultural stagnation took a while to cause problems on a planet where occasional outbreaks of civilized behavior briefly flourish, before being extinguished by the human savagery around them. In short, Earth is a bad hood. By 1095 the Christian Empire of Europe had perfected savaging its own people and Pope Urban I launched the First Crusade to wrest the Holy Land from the Moslems. Even Thomas Jefferson, as president of a fledgling nation, had to dispatch the frigate USS Constitution – Old Ironsides, to pound the Mohammedans (as Muslims were known at the time) because of their attacks on US shipping interests.

Since then, the advance of civilization around the world has exploded and the planet is a better neighborhood in places. It is a neighborhood that could use a better homeowners association though. The United Nations just does not cut it as the local condominium activist, keeping peace among us by enforcing deed restrictions, and it just isn't Uncle Sam's job. America was not founded to whip a little civilization on savages, just to protect our interests against things like savages.

In any event, on a planetary scale the followers of Mohammad were a relatively minor irritation to civilized man until the advent of a petroleum-based world economic order which shifted enormous wealth from the civilized peoples of the West into the hands of the despotic bandits who ran nomadic tribes. The previous chief occupations of these tribes were survival followed by killing anyone else in sight and stealing whatever they carried. There was equilibrium between their savagery and their ability to export that savagery. Their lacking of the latter made the former a matter of second-rate concern for most of the world.

Perhaps even more frightening than our suicidal PC marching orders that prohibit accurate application of our own language, is the unspoken recognition of the savage nature of Muslim culture amongst Muslims themselves. Western Muslims speak volumes with their deafening silence about the crimes against humanity committed by the leaders of and adherents to their faith and exercise great effort to revise not just the facts of history, but they rearrange the facts of current events!

"in the big lie there is always a certain force of credibility".

Adolph Hitler in "Mein Kampf"

"You can fool too many of the people too much of the time"

Humorist James Thurber

It was pathetically funny to watch Saddam Hussein's official spokesman "Baghdad Bob" on TV "debunking" rumors of Americans in Baghdad with the emphatic statement *"There are no American infidels in Baghdad. Never!"* Television viewers were amused by the sight of Bradley Fighting Vehicles packed with US troops practically streaming through the Downtown Baghdad intersection behind him. It was also illustrative of a general truth of Islam: lie. No matter how transparent the lie, a Muslim must lie to his enemy and you, I, and our children are his enemy.

A Muslim in battle has no choice but to lie. He has been commanded to do so by Allah, via Mohammad, in stories throughout the Qur'an. Deceiving one's enemy is a weapon of Jihad no different from a sword or a Boeing 767.

By the mid-1980's, Khomeini had created a terrorist assembly line, churning out graduating classes of anywhere from 900-1,000 murder / suicide bombers at a time. These bombers, trained with sophisticated brainwashing and other techniques perfected on condemned prisoners, were so fanatical that their own trainers could not abort a mission once assigned [8]

That of course means ....

...9/11: we knew, for 15 years, we knew

Hang on; I have not put on a tin foil hat while suggesting some sort of conspiracy. We "knew" about the coming Islamic Terror Attack in the same sense that we "knew" the Japanese were going to strike our interests somewhere close to home in the closing days of 1941. What we did not know was that it would be Pearl Harbor, Hawaii at 8:00 AM on December 7. The same sort of "knowing ambiguity" that left us open to "surprise" attack that day is what left us open to another "surprise" attack a half-century later in 2001.

Part of the radical Islamic murder / suicide bomber training from the 1980's came home to roost in the Homeland on the morning of September 11, 2001. Astonishingly the White House, the Pentagon, domestic and foreign security services and those entrusted with the security of both air travel and significant known targets were taken by surprise. The media and most of the public also seemed to be oblivious.

I say "astonishing" because I knew (and my audiences knew) that Jihadist terror camps were training murder / suicide pilots to fly aircraft, including jetliners, into selected targets a decade and a half before 9/11! Nothing new there, the Japanese fielded entire squadrons of suicide "kamikaze" pilots in the Second World War.

Given our historical experience and perspective and the extensive writings and broadcasts produced by today's Jihadists telling us almost exactly what they were going to try to do (including giving us a list of targets that included the World Trade Center), it is my opinion that 9/11 stands as perhaps the single most egregious case of criminal negligence our nation has ever suffered at the hands of our own leaders. At least until the collapse of New Orleans' levees and the botched emergency response (it took *15 months* for the city of New Orleans to set up an emergency response center after some 50-years of warnings that the levee system was inadequate to prevent the inevitable.)

The Jihadist training and intent was, and is, all public record and had been published – the declassified portions anyway. *"They" knew.* Just as they knew for a half-century that New Orleans was unprotected; they were told. They even told us (in both cases!) and they have lied and continue to lie in order to cover their incompetence, stupidity, corruption and human failing by engaging in finger pointing and partisan blame assigning, most of which involves a good deal of revisionist history. This is no conspiracy in the normal sense of the word (nobody sat down and planned all this) but is instead a predictable and preventable alignment of individual agendas and butt covering that just happen to be fellow travelers on these points.

Yossef Bodansky is one of the people who told them (and us). Bodansky is a widely published and respected researcher into Islamic terrorism. He is also the Director of the Congressional Task Force on Terrorism and Unconventional Warfare for the US House of Representatives. With extensive scholarly work and insight, he has advised government officials and the private sector for many years. In his 1993 response to the first World Trade Center Attack, he revealed to the public for the first time, the existence of an extensive murder / suicide pilot training program sponsored by Iran and run with the cooperation of Libya and North Korea.

According to Bodansky, the training program began in the very early days of the Khomeini regime. At first, it relied on explosive packed, single-engine military training aircraft but by 1983, it had grown into a fleet of aircraft that included *"25 Cessna Turbojets, some 15 Falcon Jets, and a few DC-3s."* [9]

That program, however, was simply a more highly developed variation on the old Japanese Kamikaze and not good enough for Allah. Khomeini kicked things up a notch by giving to his terrorist trainers a complete western-built international airport and outfitted it with state of the art equipment. Iran Air chipped in a little terror-training camp warming gift of 2 Boeing aircraft; a 707, a 727, and an Airbus A300. [10]

At least some of the terrorist "aircrews" were trained to hijack passenger aircraft and fly them all; passengers and hijackers into their intended targets, some *15 years before 9/11.* [11]

According to Jihadist ideology, which appears for all to avail themselves of in volumes of audio and videotapes and written diatribes to be mainstream Islamic creed, *ALL* Muslims are at war, *always*. This theme is as common in Jihadist writing as is Jew bashing, and increasingly it is being exposed more and more as mainstream Islamic thought as we researchers and journalists look further into the shadows of Mohammedan philosophy.

Heretofore, this extremism has been heralded only as a characteristic of "radical" Islam or "Islamofacism" and said to be limited to the more backward societies of the world and usually expressed in Arabic by a frothing Ayatollah. However, we are learning everyday though, that what we once classified as exotic or strange as it was dangerous is here in the Homeland, as expressed *pre-911* by a respected Islamic preacher during Friday Services, in a most unusual place: Raleigh, North Carolina.

> *"The rational Muslim should not expect to live his life in peace, hoping that his life will not be affected by the deceit, conspiracy and the oppression of the enemies. On the contrary, the Muslim should prepare himself for a long bitter confrontation, which will not cease until he meets his Lord, Allah, while he is in this conflict"* [12].

As to the nature of the conflict referenced "conflict" Muslims believe that Allah defines the enemy (speaking through Mohammad) in the Qur'an, in *surat* An-Nisa', (verse 76),

> *"Those who believe, fight in the Cause of Allah, and those who disbelieve, fight in the cause of at-taghut (Satan). So fight you against the allies of Satan; Indeed, the plot of Satan is weak."* [13]

The Million Muslim March

In the summer of 2005, the FBI broke up a suspected al Qaeda terrorist cell in the sleepy California city of Lodi. Lodi is an agricultural center along the spine of the fertile Central Valley of the Golden State. It is also home to a quiet mosque with a congregation of around 2,000 faithful. The mosque and its membership have never been anything but upstanding and respected, if somewhat cloistered and mysterious, but in that respect no more cloistered and mysterious than a Hasidic neighborhood or a monastery.

My relationship with Islamic pressure groups has always been rocky (no surprise there) and one in particular has routinely pulled out the stops to get me shut down. The Council on American-Islamic Relations (CAIR) is a mouthpiece for Islamic Terror in the United States. They are a Mecca Mary, and like Tokyo Rose before them, their job is to undermine America from within. No one from CAIR has ever personally participated in a terrorist act of any kind (at least not that I am aware of) but they are full-time apologists of Jihad and were very vocal in defending Osama bin Laden in the first few days following the 9/11 Islamic Terror Attacks [15].

Nonetheless, with the help of the Mayor of Lodi, Holly and I were able to sit down and break bread with the CAIR Northern California chapter executive director to discuss a publicly visible Islamic response beyond the whining about being singled out and picked on that invariability follows each outburst of Islamic terrorism anywhere in the world. The response we agreed upon was a community march to denounce terrorism in the name of Allah. It would be called the "Million Muslim March" and the entire community would be invited to participate and then attend an interfaith event at a central location. The name of the event was simply a play on words. Realistically we anticipated a turnout anywhere from the dozens to hundreds; either result would have been reassuring.

"Reassuring" didn't turn out to be the word… the word that best fits is more like "reaffirming."

With the help, of what was now *national* publicity, I got three, exactly three Muslims; the guy from CAIR, the Imam of the Lodi Mosque and an Islamic-Egyptian businessman from Sacramento. Three Muslims ready to stand with the Mayor of Lodi, my wife and me, to denounce those who would "hijack" the Religion of Peace and turn it into a savage weapon.

The total Muslim population in the Lodi – Sacramento corridor is roughly 40,000.

I have since learned that a similar effort had been made the previous May in Washington, DC. The moderate Muslim group that tried to stage the event on the National Mall and involve the maximum possible number of Muslims in the country, had managed to attract a total of fifty people [16] – total, from the entire Muslim population of the United States of America, and we have no idea how large that number is.

Estimates of the number of Muslims in the US run from a low of 1.6 million to a high of 12 million [17]. According to Yossef Bodansky, whatever the number, it includes thousands upon thousands of "sleeper" terrorists just like the 9/11 gang, awaiting the call to unleash their unholy, human-sacrifices to their twisted faith [18].

The common refrain, especially in the hyper-charged politically correct sewage that pollutes clear thinking, is that all of this is some lurid fantasy, from twisted minds intent on "hijacking" Islam. Fine choice of a word actually, former President Bush used it himself in the very same context. Too bad it's wrong.

What does Islam have to say about "moderate" Muslims who seek peace? Try this on for size:

"The enemies of Allah are in our midst. They claim to be Muslims, although they are as far as can be from Islam. They call themselves 'reformists' or 'preachers,' and say that we support the West. They are hostile to us on these grounds…if we do not stop all the transgressors who are trying to distort Islam with their claims of reform and their corrupt progress - this will be dangerous. These people have been tempted by the West, and have been employed in its service. We are familiar with their relations with foreign elements. We are fighting them and will continue to fight them, and we will cut off their tongues."

That charming little ditty comes from our *friend* Saudi Interior Minister Prince Nayef bin Abd Al-'Aziz and is excerpted from a much longer puke [19] that he directed toward those Muslims whom he considers to be "tools" of the "enemy" (that would be us).

My point is not that Muslims are bad people. This is not a call to alarm us to repel an invader, nor is it a belittling of any culture, faith, or person. It is simply a statement of fact that Islam encourages a dangerous and backward worldview. The impact of that stagnated culture previously held at bay by equally backward economic, social, and technological systems rooted firmly in a time far before the Industrial Revolution strives to remain frozen in time at the point where Mohammad had his psychotic break. That savage throwback worldview from medieval times has suddenly been thrust into the Jetson's world of the 21st Century, and Islam is grotesquely unprepared to cope.

And now they are building Nukes with, at best, tepid opposition from the rest of the world and while a United States President named Hussein watches.

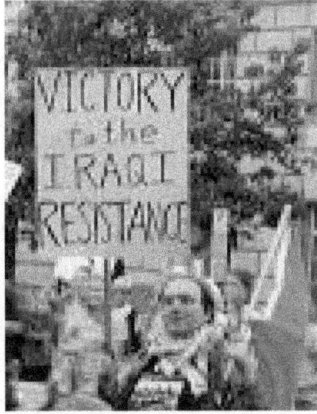

Politically correct = suicide

"Islamic terror plot to blow US flagged jetliners out of the sky over the Atlantic Ocean!" is always a fun headline to wake up to. Especially on a day when you are waking up in a terrorist's dream target of Washington, DC and later that same day flying out of Dulles International Airport (on the terrorists' top ten list for sure) on a cross-country flight to Sacramento (terrorists love those cross-country flights; all that fuel makes for a really spectacular fireball).

That is the position my wife Holly, my then 12-year old daughter Danielle, Casey the Pound Dog and I were in when legendary stiff upper British lips crushed a large-scale terrorist attack on civilian flights originating in London and bound for US destinations in the summer of 2006.

After a week in the District, we were accustomed to the living resurrection of Blitz-era London style security. Oh sure, concrete barriers have replaced sandbags around public buildings and quaint air raid wardens have been replaced by beefy, heavily armed robo-cops, any one of which could single-handedly suppress a small insurrection. But, this New Blitz USA is essentially the same mixture of caution, precaution, outright fear, and total confusion about how to enact actual security that England must have endured.

Not to worry, the man behind the curtain has everything under control. Then we got to the airport. Imagine my surprise at encountering a Transportation Security Administration (TSA) security screener wearing her hijab as she culled through peoples' bags in the secondary search area at Dulles.

Far be it from me to suggest that a Muslim woman not be allowed to wear her traditional headscarf on the job but it is perfectly within my rights to question the job upon which the hijab was being worn. A Muslim, screening for Muslim terrorists at one of the most sensitive security choke points in the country's air travel system? Something wrong with that picture? Maybe just a little? To pick just a random concern; given that Allah would surely frown upon her in a confrontation with a true believer intending mayhem, one wonders just how far political correctness and tokenism must be taken.

The mental game I played with myself to deal with this was to reach the hopeful conclusion that this nice lady was the contemporary equivalent of an Indian Scout working with the Cavalry to track down the bad Indians. Just the same though, a disturbing thought kept intruding – that the more accurate analogy might be German saboteurs dropped on a Long Island, New York beach by a U-Boat in 1942 and later captured and executed before they could act. *Should I grab this woman and call a cop?* I wondered. Nope.

She *is* a cop, of sorts, and that means that the cops have been compromised and cannot be trusted (cue the Oath Keepers!).

Great. The terrorists want us dead; the chief value of the TSA to this point has been to enable the airlines to abuse their customers beyond the airlines' wildest dreams and is now apparently also tasked with making sure that when we do go down, it is in an infidel rainbow ball of flame, all-inclusive and politically correct. Because, that after all, is what happens when you hold a guy like Uncle Sam down and castrate him with those PC scissors.

If there is nothing wrong with Muslims; there must be something wrong with Islam

I must however close this chapter with the reminder that it is ideology under discussion here, not a people – and an admonition to those who would twist my words to reflect otherwise. The point is fine, the line is fuzzy, and the moral dilemma we Americans face trying to reconcile our concepts of equality and right with the reality that good people are easily forced into horrible and inhumane actions is agonizing.

A very sincere attempt must be made when examining our actions and thoughts to not confuse morale lifting propaganda (which is frequently heavy in dehumanizing images of the humans who comprise the enemy) with our reality that in the end it is the offending system and not the people who are loathsome. Indeed, the people who live under the systems seeking our destruction are the true victims. They are victims, lied to and indoctrinated by their "leaders' into the belief that we are the evil in this world. That is because those systems and the people who benefit from them realize that if the people ever actually tasted individual rights and achieved even a full belly that those systems – including radical Islam – would fracture and crumble like that perverted, oppressive house of cards that they are.

I can find no better popular culture illustration of the moral conundrum facing us than the following dialogue from one of the Second World War's finest works of the fine art of boosting morale while efforting to separate the "enemy" from the system that victimized them.

In this dialogue, taken from the classic 1943 Warner Brothers Film "Destination Tokyo," the language is very politically incorrect and contains what is now considered a derogatory racial slur toward Japanese people. However, if you put aside your well-earned politically correct lenses and pay attention to the underlying message, you can easily see that even then, in the prehistoric days before PC, that Americans struggled with balancing national survival with national principle.

In this scene, Cary Grant, playing the role of submarine USS Coperfin Captain Cassidy, refers to a sailor named "Mike," who had been stabbed in the back by a Japanese soldier. The story of Mike is a metaphor for the Attack on Pearl Harbor and the painful reconciliation of our rage, our national peril, and America's moral torture. I have reproduced the dialogue verbatim as published in "*Screening the Past*":

> "*I remember Mike's pride when he bought the first pair of roller skates for his five-year old boy. Well, that Jap got a present when he was five too, only it was a dagger so he'd know what he was supposed to be in life. The Japs even have a ceremony that goes with it. At seven a Jap kid is taking marches under an army instructor, at thirteen he can put a machine gun together blindfolded. So, as I see it, that Jap was started on the road twenty years ago to putting a knife in Mike's back. There are lots of Mike's dying right now and a lot more Mike's will die until we wipe out a system that puts daggers into the hands of five-year-old children. You know, if Mike was here to put it into words right now, that's just about what he died for. More roller skates in the world, including some for the next generation of Japanese kids, because that's the kind of man Mike was.*" [20]

In the end, in real life "Mike" (America) made sure that the next generation of Japanese kids, and many more would have roller skates and not daggers on their fifth birthday. If we do not lose our courage and stop kowtowing to political correctness than the next generation of Muslim kids may have iPods instead of belt bombs.

It is not wrong, it is not racist, it is not intolerant to look evil in the eye and call it evil. It is a matter of survival. Nonetheless, be forewarned that evil will retaliate and it knows how to hurt you. It knows that you are good; it knows that you are in agony to look at someone and think that "they" are an "enemy"; it knows the power of using your own goodness against you. It will not kill you it will do worse. It will label you "politically incorrect," "right wing," or some other hideous modern version of a yellow Star of David. Wear your label proudly because it means you are thinking for yourself and not allowing your own insecurities over how others view you to dictate the direction of your moral compass or your ability to recognize truth. But do not ever allow someone to label you a racist because you recognize the enemy when you see him.

---

[1] *Target America and the West: Terrorism in the U.S. Today*, by Yossef Bodansky, Shapolsky Publishers, New York, 1993, paperback edition, p.1.

[2] Ibid, p 4,

[3] Ibid, p 2-10

[4] Ibid, p 1

[5] *The Quranic Concept of War*, by Brigadier S.M. Malik, Pakistan, 1979, p 59

[6] Bodansky, *Target America* , p 9-10

[7] *Dictionary.com Unabridged (v 1.0.1)*. Based on the Random House Unabridged Dictionary, © Random House, Inc. 2006.

[8] Bodansky *Target America*, p 13

[9] Ibid, p 14

[10] Ibid, p 15

[11] Ibid, p 17

---

[12] *"The Enemy of Man"* Friday sermon delivered by Imam Mohamed Baianonie at the Islamic Center of Raleigh, NC on August 28, 1998,

recoverable at: http://islam1.org/khutub/Enemy_of_Man.htm & *Will Islam Be Our Future? A Study of Biblical and Islamic Eschatology*, by Joel Richardson, ch 16, pub by Answering-Islam dot Org, USA 2006, recovered from http://www.answering-islam.org/Authors/JR/Future/index.htm

[13] *"The Enemy of Man"* Friday sermon delivered by Imam Mohamed Baianonie at the Islamic Center of Raleigh, NC on August 28, 1998, recoverable at: http://islam1.org/khutub/Enemy_of_Man.htm

[14] *"Muhammad (SA) The Messenger of Allah"* Ahlul Bayt Digital Islamic Library Project 2000 – 2006, recovered from: http://www.al-islam.org/kaaba14/2.htm

[15] *"The CAIR-Terror Connection"* by Joe Kaufman, Front Page Magazine, April 29, 2004

[16] *Militant Islam Monitor*, http://www.militantislammonitor.org/article/id/610 , May 15, 2005

[17] *"How many Muslims are there in the US and the rest of the world"*, Religious Tolerance dot Org, by Ontario Consultants on Religious Tolerance, retrieved from: http://www.religioustolerance.org/aboutus.htm

[18] Ibid, Bodansky *"Target America"*, p 10-17

[19] Speech by Saudi Interior Minister Prince Nayef bin Abd Al-'Aziz, which aired on Al-Majd TV on September 25, 2006, translation and audio/video of original source recovered from: http://memri.org/bin/articles.cgi?Page=subjects&Area=jihad&ID=SP130506

[20] *"Screening the Past"* by Tony Barta Greenwood Publishing 1998 P 90

The author (center) with troops from the California Army National Guard at Saddam's Palace of the Four Heads in Baghdad

Illegal immigration

I f we are to engage in a discussion about illegal immigration, then it is critical that in whichever language we conduct that debate, we agree to use the commonly accepted definitions of specific words in that language.

For our purposes, the language will be Americanized English and there are four simple words. The meanings of these four words (the ideas behind them) are as exceedingly simple as they are surgically precise.

Opponents of immigration reform habitually muddy the debate by purposely ignoring the definitions of the four words in question. They do this because it opens the door for them to once again wield the most devastating Weapon of Mass Disruption in the darkest closets of demagoguery: race. If sensible immigration policy and reasonable border security can be framed as an issue of race, in this case Hispanic and Latino being cast in the role of being sent to the back of the bus, then any meaningful dialogue that may lead to a solution is impossible.

The first word is "Immigrant" and it describes a person who moves his legal residence from one sovereign nation to another. It is not necessary that an immigrant shed his birth citizenship and adopt US citizenship, only that the individual arrive and reside here in compliance with applicable immigration law. In short, an immigrant is a foreigner who lives in the United States with our permission and in accordance with whatever restrictions or privileges that accompany such permission and is not part of the issue.

The word that causes call the consternation to the enemies of common sense is: "Illegal." Are we all on the same page here? For those liberals reading this the word "illegal" means "no." Illegal means not legal, against the law, the man will oppress you to the pokey. Got it?

Finally the word "Alien" comes into play here as well. With all due apologies to George Noory, there are only two kinds of aliens, both terrestrial. They are those foreign nationals who are in our country. At any given time there are several hundred thousand of them here on any one of more than 240 different kinds of visas offered by the United States.

The United States of America has more keys to the front door for foreign nationals to enter our homeland than any other country on Earth. Let that sink in for a second. No other nation on Earth has more different pretexts for entry than do we. These aliens are here with our permission, enjoy all applicable privileges, and abide by all pertinent restrictions

The second group of aliens is far larger. Some estimates put the number as high as twenty million but if you look into numbers offered by the mainstream immigration reform organizations, you will see that they all agree, more or less, that the number is less than that, but more than ten million.

You arrive at the words for this second group by combining the words "illegal" and "alien." An "illegal alien" is a foreign national, of no particular nationality – he is not a US citizen, who is in this country without our permission.

Here is the analogical exercise for the liberal still trying to get hip to the scene. See if you can pick from the two examples below, which most closely describes the concept behind "illegal alien."

Example #1: A stranger appears at your front door and asks to come in. You ask why. He says that he has just heard that you have a nice house and he would like to see it. You invite him in on the condition that he remove his shoes and stay only until dinner because you have company. The stranger takes off his shoes, comes in, sees your home, and leaves before dinner.

Example #2: Same as in Example #1, only in this example the stranger decides that going to your front door involves more effort than he is willing to exert, not to mention that going to the front door carries the risk that you might say "no." Instead, the stranger goes around to the back and climbs in the bathroom window. His shoes track mud through your house as he takes his tour and when dinnertime rolls along he helps himself to a plate and demands to use the television remote control. You, of course, object and call the police. When the police respond they scold you for being intolerant and hogging all the good life for yourself.

The line of perfect strangers lining up at the front door to ask our permission to be in our home grows longer by the second, and as frustrated as any American, as they watch a torrent of other perfect strangers pouring in through that bathroom window, the back door, the basement,….any hole big enough to squeeze through. They also get to watch with us the spectacle of United States law enforcement officers protect the criminal, at the expense of the honest.

Heather MacDonald is a senior fellow at the Manhattan Institute for Policy Research, a think tank in New York City. She analyzed illegal immigration for *City Journal* and the *Los Angeles Times* and testified before a congressional committee on the scope of the criminal element that has replaced the stereotype of a hard working guy with a strong back and noble heart who just wants to pick those grapes for that buck.

Among many other sunning revelations, Mac Donald stated that:

- *"The leadership of the Columbia Lil' Cycos gang, which uses murder and racketeering to control the drug market around Los Angeles' MacArthur Park, was about 60 percent illegal in 2002. Francisco Martinez, a Mexican Mafia member and an illegal alien, controlled the gang from prison, while serving time for felonious reentry following deportation."*

- *"In Los Angeles, 95 percent of all outstanding warrants for homicide in the first half of 2004 (which totaled 1,200 to 1,500) targeted illegal aliens. Up to two-thirds of all fugitive felony warrants (17,000) were for illegal aliens."*

- *"The Los Angeles Police Department arrests about 2500 criminally-convicted deportees annually."*

The researcher also testified that law enforcement studies in California, going back to 1995, estimate that as many as sixty-percent of our street gangsters are illegal aliens. [1]

Astoundingly enough, when faced with undisputed wave of violent crime attributable to a clearly identifiable population, most law enforcement agencies in the state practice, at best, "catch and release" with illegal aliens. The beleaguered LAPD (Los Angeles Police Department) is further hamstrung by a bizarre concept known as "Sanctuary Laws" that prohibit local law enforcement agencies from enforcing immigration laws. In Massachusetts, newly elected governor Deval Patrick (D-far left even for that state) announced that as one of his very first priorities upon taking the oath of office would be to declare his entire state an illegal alien free fire zone by ordering state law enforcement to ignore all immigration related laws! [2]

Such laws came into vogue during the Reagan years when that president led this nation on an aggressive campaign to protect our national interests. That campaign resulted in the eventual fall of the Soviet Empire but some of you will also recall that there was as much effort to secure our interests in our own hemisphere as there was in tearing down the Iron Curtain.

A consequence of that was that commie rats began abandoning socialist ships (revolutions) all over this side of the world. Many, if not most of those commie rats, came to the United States and sought refuge with the American left, which is nothing more than a more sophisticated version of Marxism. To "protect" these enemies of America from America liberals forced through these so-called sanctuary laws. Originally, an expansion of an existing notion, namely political asylum, the objective was expanded to include asylum from prosecution for crimes against this country and humanity.

Los Angeles and San Francisco were two cities that quickly adapted the idea to their own even further left, bizarre cultures and essentially declared all criminals off-limits to law enforcement, provided the criminal is of a protected class or commits a politically acceptable crime - illegal aliens being the protected class and their crimes politically correct.

The law & order arguments advanced by conservatives are plain enough and speak for themselves. I do not however argue solely from that perspective, rather illegal immigration ignites my empathy and offends my sense of justice and humanity because exploiting the desperation of others is just plain wrong.

About those "jobs Americans won't do"

Help Wanted, Napa Valley - day laborers $875.00 - $1,025.00, Includes accommodation, and supper.

No, that's not what the job pays. *That is what you pay them!* [3]

No fake Jake.

The concept is labeled "Crush Camp" and involves groups of Yuppies who pay $875.00 for a day ($1,025.00 for two days) picking grapes. The idea started in California and like most bad infections from California, Crush Camp is spreading unabated across the nation. I even found one in Ohio, a place where one drinks wine by grasping it firmly by the middle of the brown paper bag.

In California, so many Americans are lining up to pay royally to do this particular job that Americans won't do that one of the largest operators in the state, Diageo, has had to slap a twenty-five Yuppie limit on enrollment! That's right; they are turning away people who wish to pay a cool grand to do a job that ordinarily pays around $2.00 per bucket.

That $2.00 a bucket only applies if you speak Spanish, are brown, and happen to need the gig in order to try to buy your wife and daughter back from your coyote's sex dungeon or to cover your payments to the nice human and drug traffickers from the notorious MS-13 (Mara Salvatruch) street gang.

If somebody can get a thousand bucks just for the grape-picking thing just imagine what we could get for the full treatment! I'm waiting for the "Cotton pickin' plantation weekend" to catch fire in some place like Mississippi. At the end of the day we could sit around the hangin' tree, sing old Negro Hymnals and play "Dodging the overseer's whip."

Those of you paying grape pickers who opt to overnight and displace illegal aliens - excuse me, migrant laborers doing a job that Americans won't do - for a second day will also enjoy a fine "Harvest meal." Your day, says the brochure, promises you the same "beautiful vistas" of Napa Valley and the Golden Gate Bridge that the regular pickers get to see (from their cardboard boxes) each night as they enjoy their own harvest meal.

Where are the bleeding hearts? Conservatives are fighting so hard to end the abuses of illegal immigration and the powerful interests that exploit illegals that they have torn their own party down the middle. Here is a perfect example of conservatism trying to be compassionate and having to fight the cold, heartless exploiters of the oppressed under-classes all by their lonesome.

What happened to "No justice, no peace!" and "United, the people can never be defeated!"? This oppression has it all! People of color, people politically and economically disadvantaged, people discriminated against in their own countries and abused here, human rights offenses.... pick a liberal touchstone and tell me that it's not red hot from all the action on just this issue!

I guess that liberals just have too much money and too many grapes to pick on a lark to care about the swelling human rights atrocities associated with our return to a pre-13th & 14th Amendment economic model, coupled with a whining narcissistic excess from some quarters that makes ancient Pompeii look reserved by comparison.

All of this is building up to my most fundamental point on illegal immigration: it (illegal immigration) is a sinister, neo-pre-Emancipation Proclamation exploitation of people driven to desperation by their circumstances. The current state of affairs surrounding humans being bought sold and rented in or for the US market is a human rights atrocity. We're watching the plantation owners' swap out Africans for Latinos - no difference but for the lack of visible chains. Supporters of illegal immigration are really saying that they support the exploitation of the desperation of people of a different skin color and who speak a different language.

The US State Department annually issues a report on the world slave trade. [4] The 2006 report looked at some eight-dozen nations around the word. These reports have a treasure trove of details that paint a depressing picture of the illegal immigration problem as a wide-scale human rights abuse. However, the report climbs up on a politically correct high horse and excludes the United States of America from its own report. The 2002 report pegged the number of slaves worldwide at between seven hundred thousand and four million. They included in the definition of "slave" those unfortunate souls in indentured servitude and non-custodial forced labor, like in the textile sweatshops of New York City and the whorehouses of San Francisco.

That is quite a spread. Do we have a handle on the numbers here?

No. I have seen numbers in various periodicals and news items that briefly flash through the news cycle or that are forwarded to me by advocacy groups on all sides of the issue. The only number I have been able to pin somebody down on, is a number given by Colin Powell.

In announcing the 2002 annual report on the world slave trade, then Secretary of State Powell only hinted at the scope of the problem when he said that *fifty-thousand* men, women and children are sold into just the illicit sex trade alone in the United States of America, and that number is *annually!* Of the balance: *"Here and abroad,"* [said Powell] *"the victims of trafficking toil under inhuman conditions -- in brothels, sweatshops, fields and even in private homes."* [5]

On December 12, 2006 federal officials raided a Swift & Company meatpacking plant in Greeley, Colorado as part of "Operation Wagon Train." By the time the "train" pulled out of Greeley, it had 1,200 suspected illegal aliens on board for the trip to holding and then to the border. "Operation Wagon Train" [6] had been chugging along quietly like a minimized program running in your Windows® operating system.

Raids by Immigration and Homeland Security people had been reported sporadically throughout 2005 and 2006, but this particular raid is significant because of the unusual step taken by the mainstream "old" media in reporting what followed, and what followed puts the final nail into the coffin in which now rests the myth of illegal immigrants being necessary because "Americans won't do" certain jobs – like working in a meatpacking plant.

The line of LEGAL immigrants and US Citizens formed quickly and by the next morning snaked out the employment office doors and onto the street. [7] Swift & Company hadn't advertised openings but the immigration raids had made big news in Greeley. Greeley, according to the US Department of Labor [8] enjoyed, at the time, a relatively low average, seasonally adjusted unemployment rate of 4.0% yet, even in the face of a number that economists call "Full Employment," Americans still lined up out the door in the hopes of landing one of those jobs that American's won't do.

Among the hundreds of illegal aliens and illegal immigrants arrested in Greeley (and roughly hundreds more in simultaneous raids in a number of Midwestern cities) were suspects in crimes connected to their illegal status; thievery, identity theft and other related charges.

Not unexpected either, was the left wing PC Police who immediately saturated the rest of the mainstream media and the blogosphere with incendiary characterizations of both law enforcement and the criminal aliens rounded up: "Victims" screamed eCanada.Now; ultra-Left Info-News.com and other far left (and socialist) web sites alleged "racial profiling."

One blogger went so far as to bemoan the "poor families" suddenly finding pop missing in action (on a bus to the border) and cried *"what will the children do?"* A better question, unaddressed by the Left, is *"What kind of man would put his family in such jeopardy by engaging in a life of crime?"* Sure I feel sorry for the families. I feel sorry for the families, especially the kids, of most bums, creeps, and criminals, when the "bread-stealer" gets caught and marched off to the pokey. It sucks for everybody all around.

Those who would undermine your family and our nation count on your empathy. You are a good person, so am I. We feel horribly that of more than 6-billion souls on this Earth, only a few hundred million of them live in relative security and comfort, and most of those live in the United States. We all know that but for an accident of birth and divine blessings that it could be us and our families waiting for a bag of rice to be dropped out of a United Nations C-130, and we give thanks every day that we are not.

Among the many good things that make us, it also makes us an easy mark for the hucksters of the Left who exploit that goodness and misdirect our sympathy to the criminal.

On this issue, there can be no dispute over what is right and what is wrong from either the Left or the Right.

---

[1] Testimony of Heather Mac Donald, Senior Fellow, Manhattan Institute for Policy Research, before the House Judiciary Subcommittee on Immigration, Border Security, and Claims, Washington, DC, April 13, 2005. Recoverable at: http://www.manhattan-institute.org/html/mac_donald04-13-05.htm

[2] *"Gov: Staties won't grab illegal aliens"*, by Casey Ross, The Boston Herald, January 12, 2007.

[3] *"Travel: It's Camp Chardonnay"* Newsweek Magazine, New York, September 13, 2006 issue.

[4] 2006 Report *"Victims of Trafficking and Violence Protection Act of 2000: Trafficking in Persons Report"* United States Department of State, June 2006, recoverable at: http://usgovinfo.about.com/gi/dynamic/offsite.htm?site=http://www.state.gov/g/tip/rls/tiprpt/2002/10678.htm

[5] *"Modern Slavery: People for Sale: person-trafficking – a global problem"* About dot com / US Gov Info, by The New York Times Company, New York, recoverable at: http://usgovinfo.about.com/library/weekly/aa061202a.htm

[6] US Department of Immigration and Customs Enforcement, Fact Sheet, December 12, 2006, revised December 26, 2006, recovered from: http://www.ice.gov/pi/news/factsheets/061212wagontrainfs.htm

[7] *"Loss for one is another's gain"*, by Fernando Quintero, Rocky Mountain News, December 15, 2006, Denver, Colorado

[8] U.S. Department of Labor Bureau of Labor Statistics, recoverable from http://www.bls.gov/eag/eag.co_greeley_msa.htm#Fnote2

Voting

The almost mystical status granted our voting privileges as Americans escapes me. A novel and unique concept at its conception, the idea that the citizenry should have a say in its own political and social fate was revolutionary, quite literally, as the British soon learned at Lexington Green. We have embraced expansion of that idea to include all adult citizens. In fact, we have never limited the right to vote to just citizens.

We tend to think of citizenship as being a prerequisite for suffrage rights that is not now and has not been true. Until 1926 some 22 states and an unknown number of localities at one time or another provided for aliens, otherwise in compliance with voting requirements, [1] including two original colonies; Vermont and Virginia, at the beginnings of the nation [2].

Non-citizen voting fell out of vogue when Southerners blamed Abraham Lincoln's election on ballot box stuffing by immigrants, most of whom opposed slavery. A general anti-immigrant fever swept the United States in the last years of the 19th century and the first decades of the 20th, which led to the barring of non-citizens voting in most of the nation.

Beginning with the women's suffrage movement, and then with a full head of steam cooked up during the Civil Right's era, the practice saw a revival in the later half of the 20th and first years of the 21st Centuries. Communities across the nation to allow not only legally compliant non-citizens vote in local elections (usually things like school boards and other local bodies and issues) [3] but a drive of unknown proportions to involve illegal aliens in our electoral process as voters is currently under way. Advocates of "immigrant rights" are successfully promoting the idea that citizenship is irrelevant to one's status as a voter [4].

In an echo from the Confederacy, conservative Republican Congressman, Robert Dornan, blamed the immigrant vote for his 1996, 984-vote loss to Democrat Loretta Sanchez in conservative Orange County, California. In Dornan's case, the immigrants in question were illegal immigrants. Dornan took his case to the full congress, which rejected his argument, and then to the voters of Orange County again in a 1998 bid for his old seat. [5]

He lost.

Voting is not a right nor is it an absolute duty of citizenship

Too many otherwise intelligent and attentive citizens hold the opinion that voting is not just their right and their responsibility but that it is also the full extent of participation necessary to keep our Republic healthy.

Nothing could be farther from the truth.

Our "right" to vote is only implied in the Constitution. As written, the citizenry had little in the way of individual suffrage. A voter had to be a property owner and a free man (with the operative word being "man"). US Senators were appointed by the various state legislatures (changed to popular vote by the 17th Amendment in 1913) and the president elected by a board of electors.

To this day, the president is still elected by electors, which is why a candidate can win the popular vote but still not win the office. Our system is set up that way on purpose to negate the impact of the uneducated, the foolish, or those prone to treachery from riding a demagogic wave to a populist victory.

The system was rigged by Madison, Jefferson, et al to prevent the likes of Al Gore, John Kerry, and such fools from being swept into the highest office in the land based on promises of riches to those who have none, stolen from those who have riches earned. Under the United States Constitution, your vote is technically only advisory.

Amendments and tradition unique to our forbearers (handed down to us) evolved into the system that we employ today and which both gives each of us a little more power. Regrettably these changes have also increased the power of those demagogues. Stung by their loss in 2000 they twisted the splendid and perfect workings of the Constitutional process and portrayed that process as anti-democratic. As if discovering the concept of a Republican form of government – a democratically selected representative form of government - they screamed the slogan "ONE MAN, ONE VOTE!" as if it were a bayonet and they were the cavalry riding to the rescue of an oppressed populace.

American tradition holds that localities held democratic elections to decide issues. That is a very messy system. In New England, the practice of town meetings still lingers. Having attended a couple of those in my early years, I am here to tell you that I have been besieged by angry mobs in the streets with far more cohesion and sense of fairness. It can be a vicious and tough room. Nevertheless, the idea behind the New England Town Meeting is solid and it is the living ancestor to the system under which we mostly govern ourselves today.

We turn out to elect (hire) others to do what has become a very specialized profession of governing our various political entities. However, to conclude that decisions are made at the ballot box is not only wrong it is dangerous.

The extremists have taken over our elections

When you cast your vote on Election Day, you are usually only ratifying decisions already made. It cannot have escaped your attention that the 2008 Presidential Race began in earnest even before the votes had been counted for the 2006 mid-term elections. Some say the race for 2008 began after the 2004 reelection of George W. Bush.

In reality the race for 2008 began long before that and political machines are already positioning their champions (or wholly owned lackeys and stooges) for 2012 and beyond.

The 2008 Election saw massive voter fraud and races decided by slim votes. Those who waited until Election Day were limited to choosing between two tickets selected for them. To vote but not be part of the process that leads to that vote is a useless exercise in symbolism over substance. A major Socialist-Democrat-Obama goal is to substitute the ritual for the meaning. Breeding the apathy that comes with that is critical for their larger goals of creating dependency and destroying free initiative and thought.

I have never once accomplished a thing at the ballot box. On the other hand, by involving myself (and usually my audience) I have had a hand in the creation of new law at the local, state, and national level. My audiences and I have had major roles in the elimination of offensive policies (and even of offensive politicians and political appointees). I have helped launch candidacies and I have helped scuttle candidacies. Each and every time the issue at hand was settled long before that issue reached the ballot box – when we *allowed* them to get that far.

In the real world, issues of massive gravity and frivolity alike are decided over a dinner, in an office, while playing golf or anywhere else that is not a polling place. The old saying about the world being "run by those who show up" is absolutely gospel.

Advocates for the Socialist Agenda understand this as well as does the professional political apparatus. That is why they are active on all fronts. They work the culture wars by vigilantly monitoring entertainment media for politically incorrect thoughts and have Astroturf pressure "groups" (usually existing only on the World Wide Web) ready to swing into action in order to sanitize those instances of clear thought that come to their attention. They hold staged "grass-roots" meetings and buttonhole influential people in the community. Mailing lists and bank accounts are amassed and multiple web sites frequently set up to give which ever movement is in play the appearance of being far larger and fiercer than the reality.

The choices we face at the polling station are the distilled product of all the efforts and input from conception to ballot. That is why you find yourself not voting "for" a candidate so much as you find yourself going to the polls to vote "against the other guy." The choices have been made by the most active in the process. The most active are the most motivated. It is almost a universal truth that the most motivated are the most extreme.

The rest of us tag along, inundated by opinion polls commissioned by the media in lieu of journalism (journalism requires work). The politicians are only too happy to have the Fourth Estate asleep at the wheel or otherwise distracted because the poll taking the results offers the politicians a very valuable prize.... a foolproof formula to fool fools.

Humorist H.L. Mecken once said that a demagogue is *"one who preaches doctrines he knows to be untrue to men he knows to be idiots."* Opinion polls combined with focus groups and other tried and proven Madison Avenue techniques provide the demagogue with the exact wording he needs and how to parrot back that wording in a way effective to his advantage.

Mecken was wrong about one thing; we are not 'idiots." Well, okay, not all of us are idiots, but that doesn't mean the concept is inoperative. We encounter it every day in advertising and most of us have fallen for it at one time or another. As a kid, I can remember sending my cereal box tops off to an enchanted land known as Battle Creek and then waiting breathlessly for the coveted wonder toy that I ate all that sugar to obtain. The return mail always brought the real life version of Ralphie's Ovaltine Lil' Orphan Annie Secret Decoder Ring from Gene Shepard's "Christmas Story."

Demagogues sing the same siren song as did the pitch on the cereal box. Your vote is the box top and the demagogue installed in office is straight from one of Gene Shepard's nightmares.

By way of example, I offer this experience from my own career, involving efforts by one radio station to promote my program.

My program often involves a great deal of services to the community. My listeners have raised hundreds of thousands of dollars in charity, responded to community needs at my urging, and been involved with me in countless worthy efforts. My program is also sometimes quite acerbic and cuts no slack for the deliberately ignorant or just plain hopelessly stupid.

In an effort to soften the impact of the latter, one radio station decided to emphasize the former. The big broadcast company in question is a quality company and one of the best broadcast companies in terms of treating their own people well and in dedication to the communities in which they own properties.

They are also research fiends and do nothing without carefully researching, planning, and bench testing every idea first. In my case, they came up with a slogan for me. *"Mark Williams, he's a bad boy but he does a lot of good!"* The slogan played on the idea that while I piss lots of people off for lots of reasons, at the end of the day when the community or a kid need help, I am not infrequently among the first (if not the first) to jump in. The promotions director recruited a number of station staffers to record promotional statements along those lines. The end of every promotional piece aired or printed about me was the bad boy doing good slogan.

Within weeks, our own research showed that slogan coming back to us. When asked what popped into their heads first when they heard the words, "Mark Williams," people recited back the mantra we had designed - word for word. That the slogan is an accurate synopsizes of my program may or may not have been a factor. We will never know because asking and answering that question was not part of the research. It didn't have to be. So long as people believed the image and that it replaced any pre-existing impressions of my show or me was all that mattered.

In 2004, I addressed this tactic as a political issue in my Sacramento Union newspaper column in a piece I wrote about John Kerry, but this piece could just as easily be an even more fit description of Barack Obama:

> *"P.T. Barnum's legendary Fejee Mermaid exhibit lured the gullible with a picture of a goddess-like woman from the waist up, and an elegant well-finned fish from the waist down, painted to resemble a single bizarrely beautiful*

creature. What customers encountered upon paying their then exorbitant two-bit admission was a hideous, dried relic made up of half a monkey grafted onto half a large fish.

The Fejee Mermaid was of course only one of the celebrated con man's successful ventures into style over substance. Old Phineas was a veteran huckster by the time the fishy monkey joined his collection in 1842, yet even the man who famously coined the phrase about a sucker being born every minute expresses surprise in his autobiography that there were those who upon seeing the actual artifact refused to believe that the picture presented outside was not genuine. Any reality to the contrary was not to be accepted, therefore the mummified remains of monkey and fish must be denied, even as it stared back at them with cold, dead eyes. They just flat out refused to acknowledge that they had been hoodwinked!

A parallel phenomenon may be observed among people lured into Democrat presidential candidate John Kerry's tent.

That John Kerry is anything but Fejee Mermaid was laid to rest via televised debates with President George W. Bush. Worse than devoid of content, Mr. Kerry was flush with contrived pitches as he alternately suggested that the United States should: seek the approval of France before engaging in our own defense, that we should never seek any other nation's counsel; that we wrongly engaged Iraq, that we were right in having engaged Iraq; that as president he would unilaterally take on North Korean madman Kim Jung II (currently under multi-national pressure which Kerry would abandon), and that he would make the world safer by engaging us in a virtual and unilateral nuclear disarmament via attrition of our current stockpile and moratorium on the development of next generation newer, smarter and less devastating (to innocents) nuclear technology – while giving nuclear materials to the Islamic Terrorist state of Iran.

To say that Mr. Kerry is a confused man is naïve. Mr. Kerry and his team of skilled con men are no more confused than was Barnum. It is hard to look at his little group of Oompa Loompas and not see the guys who siren songed me into the old Clyde Beatty-Cole Brothers circus sideshow when I was a kid. The collections of contradictory sound bites from Mr. Kerry ring eerily familiar, like the side show professionals of my youth the Kerry Campaign Barnums: Carville, McAuliffe, Lockhart, McCurry, and Kerry himself seize on their marks and tailor their banter to each new potential sucker. All Barnum wanted was your quarter. Kerry wants the nation's soul.

Symbolic of the huckster in lieu of honest man that is Mr. Kerry is the image of him recently showing up on the trail with an artificial tan, just a shade orange short of signifying an elevation in the nation's terror alert. Metaphorically to the late Barnum's memory (and a fitting if unintended tribute to the great ringmaster) was the lie about the early autumn Nantucket sun oranging the senator during a touch football game. Such a comical story could remind one of the real JFK, or of a painting of a half-goddess half-fish, while indicating just how far or not the turnip truck has driven since dropping said observer off.

Yet disbelieving believers persist nightly on the evening news. With tones of great gravity and concern for the nation Misters Blather, Brokejaw, and The ABC Canuck recount stories of smirks, blue versus red ties, tall versus short, country style versus Gucci-clad urbanite. A four-year track record of astonishing accomplishment up against skating through a narcissistic lifetime of being a ratfink, then playboy turned gigolo, and lying and cheating is ignored while they desperately search for something to convince us that the painting is reality and the horrific lie is not.

The message here is not to blow off the next election and call my program to crab about the unsatisfactory result. Neither is it to vote, then call my program and crab about the unsatisfactory result, as much as I appreciate your calls and want to keep them coming. The message is that your vote is only the icing on a cake made by others, unless you haul yourself into the kitchen and start cooking.

Some people should not vote

Sometimes the best choice for the rest of us is if some of us don't vote at all. I personally consider it a high duty of citizenship to not vote if you are not informed and involved. If all you do is vote in the big election then all you are doing is selecting between choices offered up by the activists from the edges of each party. That is simply a gesture, a meaningless nod in the direction of representative democracy that speaks simply to your default affirmation (maybe even endorsement) of the ideas and work of extremists. If you are uninvolved up to the point of casting your vote and absent a reasonable understanding of the issues and personalities before you, please do us all a favor and stay home on Election Day.

Hijacked election

An old nemesis of sober governance has gained new currency, it is the promised "redistribution" of "wealth" from those who earn to those who do not. Like all good Marxists, Barack Obama set about on a long and determined campaign to demonize the working class as oppressors and glorify the unthinking and the parasitical classes as victims of those workers. He set himself up as the champion of the lazy and the center of a personality cult for the unthinking.

During my 6,000 mile, 35-city (12 states) speaking tour for Our Country Deserves Better PAC (I am a Vice Chairman of the conservative political action committee) in the days before the 2008 presidential election, I encountered many young adherents to the cult of Obama, yet not a one who could define their screeched words "HOPE!" and "CHANGE!" Requests for any sort of substantive explanation as to what those words meant in those individuals' heads were universally greeted by any combination of uses of the "F-word" hurled at me, charges of "racism," or perplexed looks, but always with increased decibel levels. The only missing element was even the vaguest definition of those ideas; if the word "idea" even applies to empty words shouted by someone who does not have an accompanying understanding of what those words even mean to them.

Massive crowds at Obama campaign events filled our television screens during the run up to the election. What was not reported by many of those "news" shows was that the crowds were there because in a grand redistribution of the concert wealth, they had been given free Dave Mason, Sheryl Crow or Jimmy Buffet tickets, just to name three of the high profile acts that put on free shows for the crowds. These are acts that routinely command anywhere from $50.00 to hundreds of dollars for a ticket. Some who were denied tickets claimed at the time that in order to get your free ticket you had to pledge a vote to Obama.

Barack Obama's genius was in living his entire life as a blank canvas. The empty canvas acquired detail along the way, but the artist was Obama himself and he filled in some of the blanks only by vagaries in books he wrote about himself. Obama then proceeded to cultivate symbolism sans substance. He proceeded to successfully buy votes en masse. Ignorance and vicious attacks on those who would question his substance were and are the twin weapons of Obama's deception. In the end, he rose to the presidency virtually absent any record of accomplishment (beyond an extraordinary talent for self promotion) and no voting record to speak of by which we might draw conclusions about his thinking

---

[1] *"Immigrant Voting Rights Receive More Attention"* By Ron Hayduk & Michele Wucker, in Migration Information Source, Migration Policy Institute, Washington, DC, November 1, 2004

[2] *"SHOULD NON-CITIZENS BE PERMITTED TO VOTE?"* On-line debate between Jamin Raskin and Matthew Spalding, Legal Affairs Magazine, New Haven, October 5, 2005, retrieved from http://www.legalaffairs.org/webexclusive/debateclub_ncv0505.msp

[3] Ibid footnote [1] Hayduk & Wucker.

[4] Ibid footnote [2] Raskin & Spaulding

[5] *"Conservative Firebrand Bob Dornan Blazes Comeback Trail to the House"* Gebe Martinez, Washington Post, June 3, 1998

Figure 1: One of my many honors!

Media bias

"There were days when I sat in my tent alone and gloomed with the desperate belief that it was actually possible for us to lose this war."

WWII War Correspondent Ernie Pyle [1]

The late newspaperman Ernie Pyle might not have been the first embedded journalist in the history of warfare but he ranks among the most compelling for his first-hand accounts from the frontlines. Ernie was first and foremost a humanitarian and a patriot. The two nearly always go hand in hand despite what the likes of the vapid TV drones and their print cousins in the old media would have you believe. Ernie's works and attitude were indirectly summed up at the California State Capitol during the 2004 "Believe in Freedom" 9/11 remembrance by then,

Chief Editor of the *Sacramento Union Newspaper*, Kenneth Grubbs who, speaking for the new media, said: *"I am an American first and a journalist second."*

There is no ambiguity in the words of Pyle or in the mind of Grubbs. Neither struggles with seeking and asserting a non-existent moral equivalency of those who seek to kill us, yet both are notable in that they represent what is now a fringe of American journalism.

Indeed, the word "journalism" barely applies to the old media. "News" has become the filler stuffed between commercials on TV and that which is inserted into the blank spaces between the advertisements in newspapers.

> *"[I]n such a world of conflict, a world of victims and executioners, it is the job of thinking people, not to be on the side of the executioners."*
>
> Nobel laureate Albert Camus [2]

The commercial aspect of journalism with a point of view is far from new. What is new is American journalists siding with our would-be executioners. We are, after all, a nation of patriotic capitalists with a long tradition of advocacy journalism. Undeniably, the plethora of pamphlets that served the colonists of pre-revolutionary Boston and Philadelphia were anything but neutral. What they were also was not suicidal. The role of journalist has today become one of leveling the playing field for America's enemies, of seeking out or even manufacturing arguments favoring the enemy. The myth of objectivity has morphed into one of emphasizing the merits of the other side, even when that side is a merciless blood lust.

Both the Associated Press and iconic CBS were caught red-handed during the 2004 Presidential Election manufacturing phony "news" stories designed to undermine not just the commander-in-chief, but also the nation, and, by extension, our national survival, confirming the suspicions of many Americans. They represent the new face of the old media, a face which defies Darwin by agitating on behalf of the predators among the prey. By 2008, all pretense of objectivity was abandoned by the mainstream media as they openly worked as adjuncts to the Barack Obama Presidential Campaign.

Throughout the election campaign, the right wing radio talk hosts howled daily over what they perceived to be a clear bias by the ill-defined "Mainstream Media," which is roughly defined as traditional newspaper and television news programs.

After the election one of the Mainstream Media targets of the conservative hosts' wrath, the Washington Post admitted its bias. Post Ombudsman Deborah Howell examined that paper's coverage of the presidential election over the past year and in a November 9, 2008 article titled *"An Obama Tilt in Campaign Coverage"* [3] addressed readers' charges of bias by writing:

> *"…readers have been consistently critical of the lack of probing issues coverage and what they saw as a tilt toward Democrat Barack Obama. My surveys, which ended on Election Day, show that they are right on both counts."*

There was a time in our living memory when the old media actually served this nation well by exposing the fools and scoundrels who were sending our precious blood into a Southeast Asian meat grinder.

For example, without dedicated journalists with a point of view we would never have known that late former defense secretary Robert McNamara is deserving of an epitaph consisting of a vitriolic torrent of expletives and condemnations of the aforementioned monster to the eternal fires of Hell, where he will reign side by side with bin Laden, Hitler, and the appropriate rouge's gallery of grotesque creatures spawned by Satan.

What the old media today do not understand is that to ferret out and point to the failings (and lurking monsters) of our government is one thing - patriotic, even righteous. However, to work actively at undermining our nation and her defenders while working to elevate the point of view of our assailants was not envisioned by the author of the First Amendment, Thomas Jefferson. In contrast with the past, today's actions of the old media are considered by many to constitute a traitorous collaboration with the evil that has declared war just not against America but on all civilized mankind and Human Rights as defined by our Constitution.

The old media have gone from patriotic, humanitarian Americans reporting back to the Homeland, through villain hunting skepticism, to today's cynical propagandizing on behalf of the devil in a mere blink of history's eye.

Indeed, a CNN executive revealed to the New York Times in 2003 that the 24-hour cable news network had a long-term deal with Iraqi dictator Saddam Hussein that allowed CNN to maintain a bureau in Baghdad mostly unmolested. All CNN had to do in return was to look the other way and suppress any news of human rights abuses in Iraq… or anything else that Hussein did not want known to the world [4].

The difference between guys like today's largely sorry crop and journalists like Pyle and Grubbs is that the latter distinguish the demons of Hell from the angels of Heaven on behalf of the humble mortals in between who are attempting survival while trying to sort the angels from the demons.

No longer though can we trust our media to point us to which is which. The media today present both as the same as if the eternal struggle for life and liberty were a sporting event. Not only is this stupid, untrue and dishonest…it is also both homicidal and suicidal.

> *"If you are ashamed to stand by your colors, you had better seek another flag."*

Author Unknown

Among the many nuts and fruits that enjoy full Fourteenth Amendment status in California is an odd man named Steven Pearcy. Pearcy is an über control freak, and evidently not dealing with what appear to this casual observer to be some dark and troubling issues of the Id.

The joke offered by a caller to my radio show was that if Pearcy and his wife ever have a child that it will be able to car pool to therapy with Michael Jackson's kids. Maybe a bit flip, but Pearcy has an almost reptilian air about him, with the vacant look of zealotry in his eyes and a somewhat volatile temperament that causes him to be quietly frightening. As if that is not bad enough, he and his wife are both attorneys. The wife also sits as a judge pro-tem for small claims in the Sacramento County Court System.

Pearcy specializes in using the First Amendment as the foundation for his apparent goal of redefining the standard for nuisance neighbor in the middle class Sacramento neighborhood in which he owns a part time home (he lives full time in Berkeley – big surprise).

A Palestinian Flag hangs in a window facing a Jewish neighbor's home. The flag of course represents a variety of terrorist organizations from the various Palestinian Liberation Organization (PLO) splinter groups, through Hamas and is a symbol uniting those mass murders with each other and their US allies. Each of these groups considers Jews subhuman and targeted for extinction. For a couple of years, the Pearcy home has also sported an effigy of an American solider.

Initially, the stuffed uniform and helmet were attached to a street-facing eave via a hangman's noose. A community uprising with several hundred protesters descending on the quiet neighborhood ensued. It was led by Melanie Morgan (KSFO radio in San Francisco) and me; with the invaluable help of our good friends at Move America Forward (a Sacramento based charity with the goal of promoting patriotism and public support for America's fighting men and women and their families).

The noose came off the effigy when I came up with the idea of using a favorite tool of the Left's Thought Police (the enforcers of Political Correctness) against the Pearcy's; California's draconian "hate crime" law.

In California a person is considered guilty of a "hate crime" if that person is *thought* to harbor prejudice against a whole host of categories of loosely defined groups of special people. Special as in not white, middle class, law abiding, bill paying, American males... As I (and many others) warned; the very idea of a "hate" enhancement on any crime is an Orwellian absurdity, it is the act that is a crime not the thought.

You may sit and think the most obscene and horrible racist and hateful thoughts all day long, that is your right. You do not have the right to lash out and act upon that hate however. If you punch a man in the nose that man's nose remains punched regardless of its color or sexual preference. That is the crime, the nose does not care one way or another that you punched it because of the ethnic heritage of its owner, it is a nose punched plain and simple and that is the province of Man's Law.

On the other hand, when a gift horse wanders up to you it is impolite to look it in the puss. Pearcy's gift horse was in that he gave me the opportunity to both demonstrate the danger presented by California's thought crime law *and* make Pearcy's day miserable at the same time.

Together, the dummy and the context in which it appeared to me that a reasonable person could easily conclude that the display was advocating murder for the crime of being a Jew, a Christian, or an American – or any combination of the three.

Smelled like hate to me, so I found a citizen to file a complaint with the Sacramento County District Attorney's office.

As it turns out Pearcy did not have the stomach to risk losing a criminal hate crime prosecution; it was a no win for him no matter how it ended. Had he lost that would have been bad enough, but if he had successfully defended himself that would have been worse because to do so he would also have to damage or destroy a powerful weapon against freedom that the enemies of this nation and its people are saving for another day. The law we call "hate crime enhancement" should rather be titled *"thought* crime." Presented with this Hobson's choice, Pearcy gave ground, temporarily. The dummy hung soldier came down only to reappear days later, minus the noose.

Pearcy's retaliation for this minor set back was in July 2005, and in cooperation with then California Sate Attorney General Bill Lockyer who offered to use taxpayer provided resources to sponsor a display of anti-Jewish, anti-female, and anti-US "art" in the lobby of the California Department of Justice Building.

Effigy of a hung US soldier on the Pearcy's Sacramento house

The centerpiece of Lockyer's exhibition was a childish watercolor by Pearcy of the US Flag (in the shape of the Continental United States) being flushed down a toilet. Several corporate sponsors were misled (to put it politely). Liberal dogma shares one thing with Islam – besides their hate for freedom – and that is lying. For both it is a commandment and a foundational principle of their faiths). In this case the sponsors had been lied to about the nature of the display and provided generous funding to assist they were told was a legitimate art show. The initial public backlash caused at least one of them (a major regional bank) to come onto my radio program to publicly disavow the "art" display and announce their own demands that the organizers tell the truth to the public about the nature of the free expression taking place at public sacrifice.

Melanie Morgan, Move America Forward, and I responded with an art display of our own. The art, hundreds of pieces, were provided by patriotic souls and a permit was obtained to display them for several hours, on the sidewalk in front of the attorney general's office. The response was interesting, to say the least.

First; our display was referred to, even by us, as an "alternative" view. That is a stunning notion. That expressions of patriotism, appreciation for our valiant and brave defenders; and uniquely American values of inclusion, diversity and respect for individuals, could be considered an "alternative" is astonishing, even in today's bizarre, upside down, political and social environment.

Just as surprising was the attempt by the California Attorney General to shut us down with old Soviet style tactics of intimidation and the blatant us of law enforcement officers to assist a freakish group from Code Pink (bused in from San Francisco) in threatening physical violence against the ordinary citizens including dozens of children.

Steve Pearcy's "art" sparked a demonstration

Not as surprising was that our numbers were met by equal numbers of people actively trying to censor us, whilst proclaiming the virtues of free speech. Among those numbers, was an official delegation from the American Civil Liberties Union (ACLU), screaming at the top of their lungs that we should be shut down, while oblivious to the irony of their stated purpose for being there in support of free expression. They were aided by a written statement from state attorney general, William Lockyear, who issued in the midst of the competing demonstrations (ours legal with a permit theirs not) reiterating Lockyer's endorsement of the anti-American, anti-Semitic, anti-Christian and anti-female "art" on display on the taxpayers' dime – a statement in which the state's attorney general implied that those of us there to show support for our country were *"… 'Soviet government' style censors."*

The state's top law enforcement official took things one step further and dispatched the state Department of Justice police to harass our people and (in the opinions of many present, myself included) assist the other side, which unlike us was gathered sans permit. The frothing liberals persisted in intimidation, at least one instance of unprovoked physical violence, much profanity, and the blocking of pedestrian and some vehicular traffic. A police sergeant complained to Move America Forward (MAF) that the act of physical violence was reported during my live radio reports from the event and angrily demanded that the statement be retracted.

I had witnessed the assault and it was I who reported it on the air. That it was witnessed by a uniformed Department of Justice (DOJ) cop and several people asked him to take action (he did not) was also reported by me on the air. Sarge was not a happy camper and demanded that such reports not be aired! (I was also a witness to that conversation between the sarge and the MAF executive director).

Needless to say, I made a special point to repeat my report on the air as frequently as possible and with the new added details.

While many media present (sadly including my own radio station's news department) swallowed the lie that we were there to protest a single particular work and to demand that it be suppressed, the exact opposite was the case.

We were there to counter the damage done by the official endorsement of intolerance and hate endorsed by the state agencies involved. We also intended that the message be heard that while such expressions (as Pearcy's) may have a place that they are not values that have a place in official sanction.

Engaging in the act of attempted suppression of free expression was the ACLU, the DOJ and a gaggle of smelly, unwashed freaks. The shouted obscenities, the obscene gestures, the intimidation…none of it worked. Our display and program went on and our point was made. Lost on those opposing free expression and free speech, however, was their role in making our point.

Loud, rude, enraged, humorless, frothing screams of anti-American epithets; absolute intolerance and self-righteousness all describe the unwashed losers who were there to express their hate for the host organism (America) in which they exist as parasites. They wasted no time or effort in demonstrating the truism of Michael Savage's assertion that liberalism is a mental disorder. They were anything but rational and their fury was intense.

Imagine being on a lifeboat. A small group of bullies dislike the guy driving the boat and the direction in which he is taking it. Their response is to do everything in their power to sink that boat, with all hands aboard. They start kicking holes in the bottom of the boat in order to make their point. When one of us tries to prevent them from sinking our lifeboat their response is to attack us, so we turn to the crew for assistance. However, rather than stop them from sinking the lifeboat, the first mate and members of the crew restrain the rest of us from preventing the holes from being kicked in the boat, and in fact assist in the attempt to kill us all.

Any rational person would consider those trying to sink the boat mad and those members of the crew assisting them criminal…at the very least.

What was the fate of Pearcy's watercolor of the US Flag being flushed? In the midst of our "alternative" presentation, Lockyer ordered that particular piece of "art" to be moved to his private floor where he could enjoy it without all the commotion. To the best of my knowledge, it remained in the Attorney General's office until Lockyer termed out and ran for another office in 2006.

---

[1] *Here Is Your War,* by Ernie Pyle, Henry Holt & Co 1943, USA.

[2] *The little book of Peace,* edited by Patricia Chui, Lyons Press, 2002 USA

[3 *The News we kept to ourselves,* by Eason Jordan CNN Chief News Executive, New York Times, Op Ed section, April 11, 2003

[4] *An Obama Tilt in Campaign Coverage* By Deborah Howell Sunday, November 9, 2008; Washington Post Page B06

[5] CALIFORNIA PENAL CODE SECTION 422.55, recovered from: http://www.leginfo.ca.gov/cgi-bin/waisgate?WAISdocID=03491915452+10+0+0&WAISaction=retrieve

[6] United States Senator John Kerry (Democrat, Massachusetts) speaking at a rally for California Democrat gubernatorial candidate Phil Angelides at Pasadena City College, Pasadena California, October 30, 2006, video recovered from: http://www.youtube.com/watch?v=lexdNMoweWM

Sculpture in Birmingham, Alabama commemorates the attacks on Civil Rights marchers

Never Again

Why do I bother not only beating my own head against the America-haters' brick walls, but also spend so much effort encouraging others to bang their heads up against the very same bricks, and for what appear to be small victories? Why should you bother?

There are some things that we plainly must not stand by and watch unfold.

Had I been around in the tumultuous fall of 1923, I do not know if I would have recognized the man with the pistol in a German beer hall as what he was. The streets and bars of Germany were teeming with discontents and troublemakers and there was nothing about this son of a bumbling customs official to set him apart from the rest of the riff-raff.

If I had had been there and recognized Heir Adolph Schickelgruber for what he was, would I have had the nerve to act? To speak out? If only someone had; because it was this chronically unemployed, mentally ill transient who transformed his utter lack of ambition into a virulence in search of a target. He was a clownish character then, standing with pistol in hand, vowing to the drunks around him that this would be the day that the government fell.

Adolph Schickelgruber's revolution fizzled, and the street bum went to jail for a while only to reemerge as Adolph Hitler. What's more, he emerged with what was now a bona fide resume as a "leader" of the radicals, someone who today would be touted by the Mainstream Media as a legitimate voice of dissent.

Experience hath shown that in 21st Century America the vacuous talking heads who read the "news" from their Teleprompters would likely present him as a figure of credibility, forged of hardship (rather than pointing out that he was a mental and sexual freak from a line of defective, nebbish half-wits). His allies among the Mainstream Media talking heads would be singing apologist phrases to conceal the evil of his advocacy of genocide; the same way that they aid, abet, and assist today's Hand-Maidens to Satan.

It was bad enough that the foolish and apathetic allowed Hitler, and his cadre of freaks from some twisted Darwinist nightmare to rise from the shallow end of the gene pool and engulf the entire world in war, but can you imagine what would have happened if those same indifferent dupes had continued on to undermine the noble men and women who responded to the call to arms in the defense of humanity?

Today we are again engulfed in a world war against evil, and again noble men and women have answered the call. Again they wear the uniforms of the United States of America Armed Forces. Again they are the tip of the spear. Unlike then though, the fools and uncaring have been joined and are being exploited by the malevolent.

Together, they form a malignant critical mass supported by their allies in the Mainstream Media, and they (as might be said in Las Vegas) "control the table." While the alarm sounds, these people seek to short-circuit the siren and garble the urgent message that it conveys.

Many of us recognize this peril; few of us recognize the saboteurs. They have learned to masquerade as voices of reason…or mothers feigning the sting of the tragic loss of a hero son or heroine daughter.

Among those who see the Fifth Columnists for what they are, even fewer of us are in a position to bridge the short circuit in the alarm to ensure that it is heard. We are the canaries in the coalmine, only because we have one voice among many in the mass media. With that voice, sometimes comes immense responsibility, this is one of those times, and there are (fatefully perhaps) far too few up to the task.

Melanie Morgan is up to the task, as am I. So when she headed the "You Don't Speak for me Cindy" tour from San Francisco to Crawford, Texas and asked my help the answer was a no-brainer.

Cindy Sheehan is a vile woman (yes, another one of our indigenous fruits and nuts in the Golden State) whose son died an American Hero in Iraq, killed by the terrorists he was fighting. Cindy will not rest until his memory is blackened by her own hatred.

Nicknamed "The Bitch in the Ditch" by syndicated, broadcast opinion journalist Glenn Beck, Ms. Sheehan was literally camped out (with a few hundred refugees from Woodstock and bathtubs) along a lonely road between the town of Crawford, Texas, and President George W. Bush's ranch. They were all camped out and engaged in desecrating the names of individual fallen soldiers. Melanie speaks volumes to the issue of barking moon bat Cindy Sheehan and our trip to face her in Crawford in her (Morgan's) 2006 book *"America Mourning,"* so I will temper my additional observations with brevity.

The tendency to dismiss people like Cindy Sheehan as just clownish figures on the margins of society might be less harmful, indeed – even appropriate, if not for their exceptionally well organized, and exceedingly well funded boosters.

Absent a mass platform, they simply melt among the lunatics and street entertainers in places like San Francisco's Union Square, or at Park Street Station on Boston Common. Missing the element of a means of widespread exposure, to draw attention to any one of these individuals would be to elevate them to a position of credibility far beyond that which they deserve. Lacking the amplifying effect of media, they are destined a soapbox that consists of lurking either at their local copy center running of photocopies of their "work," or in the darkest corners of the Internet. Misplaced media attention frequently elevates these nuts to a level of credibility.

Sadly, credibility is for sale and the Mainstream Media (the Old Media) are selling. Hitler's ideological cronies in America at the time did not have CNN (which admitted suppressing stories of Saddam Hussein's atrocities for over a decade in return for access to his hellish world). [6] They did not have any of the alphabet soup television networks or grand old newspapers of record to do their bidding, thus they were never able to gain any traction here.

Today Hitler and his minions would be in despot hog heaven.

Across this nation, in towns large and small, a cumulative total of several millions people have turned out into the streets to show support for our fighting men and women since the re-ignition of hostilities in Iraq, following Saddam Hussein's outrageous, dozen-year long breach of the peace in the wake of Desert Storm, which itself followed his barbaric invasion and occupation of Kuwait in 1990.

In church halls, school cafeterias, and other forums they turn out to assemble gift packages from home. They organize letter and email campaigns, supportive web sites abound, and the talk show airwaves are full to the brim with well wishes and prayers. Most are ignored or minimized (often even ridiculed) by the Mainstream Media. This lends both aid and comfort to the enemy, and undermines the morale and moral authority of our forces. It deliberately inflicts maximum emotional pain and anguish on loved ones and seeks to turn the tide of public opinion against that public's own nation and best interests.

I believe that this is the intended effect of people like Cindy Sheehan.

What mother could possibly ever bring herself to imply that her own child was a terrorist while calling her child's murderers freedom fighters? What kind of person would delight in picketing the wounded or the funerals of the fallen as does she and her trolls (or are they masters)?

What kind of sub-human would use the graves of the fallen (including her own child's) as props for photo opportunities (she refuses to allow any kind of marker at his Vacaville, California grave as well) while sporting a well-rehearsed grin (or frown, depending on the demands of the photograph)? Sheehan has done all of the above.

The answers to questions like that were all my wife, Holly, and I needed to join Melanie at Crawford, Texas and lead the "You Don't Speak for Me Cindy" caravans that brought thousands of people from all over America to stand against Sheehan.

Ms. Sheehan and the bulk of the Fifth Column in this struggle are based here in the Bay Area and Northern California. Sheehan is a local. She is (as I said on Fox News Channel) *"...urinating on her son's grave..."* and upon every grave of every fallen hero. I believe that this is her intent.

When one of our own strays that far into the dark side, it is our responsibility to pick up the mess. The soldiers are protecting us with their lives, the very least we can do to watch their backs is to speak up when they are attacked at home.

Boots on the ground and those they seek to help must never be led to fear an enemy from home more than the one that lurks around them. Sadly, Melanie, Holly, and

I learned during our earlier trip (July 2005) to Iraq, that is exactly what they fear the most.

Families at home must not be allowed to be convinced by our inaction that what they hear coming from the mouths of the finely coiffed, pretty people with nice teeth who so splendidly and completely demonstrate why we call our TV set an "idiot box" in any way, reflects reality.

History is shaped by silence as much as it is by action, perhaps more so, and never in my time on this planet has philosopher Edmund Burke's words rung more true: *"The only thing necessary for the triumph of evil is for good men to do nothing."*

Neither Holly, Melanie, nor I - or the hundreds who made the trek to Crawford with us in what became a 5-mile long convoy of vehicles from a dozen states or more – nor those who supported us along the way – will remain silent. To do so would be to strip the words "Never Again!" of all meaning – and that will not, cannot, *must not* happen on our watch.

Mark Williams speaking to a Tea Party at the USS Midway/San Diego

Figure 2 The author (right) with a local dignitary and fellow activist Lloyd Marcus (wearing hat on right) on the Stop Obama Tour - October 2008 (left) / Mark with Mississippi Lt. Governor Phil Bryant at a Tea Party Express stop in his state (right)

Congressman Joe Wilson (R-SC) with the author on the Tea Party Express

The Audacity of Obama's Audacity

bama vowed to "change the world" and he, Speaker Pelosi and Senator Reid are working hard to do just that; that is what scares me. Before even being elected President of the United States, Obama laid claim to the title of Earth Emperor. Our first clue should have been the Greek Columns at the Democrat Convention in Denver.

As President, Barack Hussein Obama Jr. has already very aggressively pursued his domestic economic agenda. Quite simply put, the Obama "vision" for you and me is enforced prohibition on reward for excellence, hard work, suffering to achieve a goal or dream, and in general forcing American workers to be the economic equivalent of a dairy cow... and NOT the California "happy" kind.

That is called "Socialism." Socialism is an economic system under which those who mooch are a protected class and those who produce are an oppressed class with not claim of their own. That kind of class of people is known as a slave class.

The sweet Irony of the potential first black president instituting a modified slavery is not lost on me. I say "modified" because while Africans could not quit their "jobs" in the cotton fields, you and I are still free to quit ours and be supported by the remaining fools who chose to participate, or starve, our choice – at least for now.

Decisions regarding our own life and death are also ours for now, however Obama has that power in his sights as well.

So-called Obamacare is essentially a version of eugenics, even genocide or perhaps an ethnic cleansing – or all three, it all depends on how it is implemented, evolves and who controls it.

Obama is seeking control over the personal health care of all Americans and is demanding that we all be delivered to him as wards of the state. Official government death counselors will swoop down like vultures upon your 65th birthday (and every 5 years thereafter) to discuss your demise. That you may reasonably be expected to live at least another 15 years or so, at increasing cost to the taxpayers, also leads to the equally reasonable notion that these counseling sessions may have more to do with selling you euthanasia than easing your path to the hereafter.

Not a single advocate of health care reform has explained what needs to be reformed, beyond how we pay for it. They explain again and again how strained, inefficient, and expensive Medicare is (as well as the veterans' health care system) yet not one has explained how massively expanding a fatally flawed system will result in "reform." The word "reform" is as meaningless in this context as were the words "hope" and "change" in Obama's campaign and enjoys the same protection from examination as did they.

Not a single advocate of Obamacare has explained how socialized medicine will control costs without rationing, which of course leads to placing a price tag on everybody like we were Minnie Pearl.

Not a single advocate of a nationalized system can explain how that it equates with anything American if it is compulsory and at the same time dictates the terms, conditions and price of all private policies so that they are identical to the government's.

A basic point being missed by everyone, opponents of Obamacare included, is that if there is anything that needs to be reformed in our health care system it is in that we must expunge the massive dose of socialism that the Left has already successfully inserted into a system where government-run and/or funded health programs abound, more frequently than not in isolation from any consideration of need or effectiveness.

Of course, we all have a right to be healthy. We have a right to eat too. In neither case is it the duty of government to facilitate those rights beyond protecting them for us; much less is the government's prerogative to force us to exercise those rights. Forcing me to submit to government enforced treatment (or prohibition from treatment) and government forced death counseling is as unconstitutional and un-American as forcing me to exercise my First Amendment Right by mandating that I attend church or write a letter to the editor while mandating the church I attend or the words I scribe.

What do you think that Obama and the Loony Left would say to a program to provide firearms to every American in order to force them to exercise their Second Amendment Rights? I think that you know the answer to that one. Why nobody in the press ventures to ask Obama questions along these lines fairly boggles the mind.

No advocate of nationalized medicine has explained how socializing the system will change how we misuse medical insurance. Insurance is for a catastrophe, your car insurance for example. You do not call the insurance company and file a claim every time you fill your tank or get a flat tire. In fact, most of us carry high deductibles to keep our costs down, yet we expect medical insurance cover the most minor of medical related issues, many of which should be out of pocket.

No advocate has explained how Obamacare will address the issue of Tort Reform and our litigious society.

Will Obamacare be shielded from lawsuits? How then shall I be made whole if butchered? In the alternative, if not shielded then will the US Treasury become a blank check for ambulance chasing lawyers at the expense of everyone?

No advocate has explained how Obamacare will be administered any more efficiently than any other government program. The Cash for Clunkers cluster mess comes to mind, but for my Leftie readers please allow me to offer up this thought:

How will you feel about socialized medicine when the people in control of it are no longer your people? How will Obamacare look to you when it is controlled by the same people who brought us Vietnam and Iraq?

(Dear normal reader... I am using those last two examples only because they are a touchstone with hippies, not as an endorsement of those hippies' delusions.)

Obama's entire economic and social policy revamping of the World hinges on enough people producing enough wealth so that it is worthwhile to confiscate and redistribute, much as has happened to the Social Security system. Envisioned as an old-age pension, it today is a catchall social welfare program backed by worthless paper. I am not even sure that the majority of recipients are even "old" for that matter. Long ago abandoned as a pension program its primary purpose now is to serve as deification numbers assigned at birth to individual Americans, something that was expressly denied by the program's creators.

The One does not propose anything new but he does propose a change and in this case it is indeed lipstick on a pig, a very old pig. Karl Marx applied the first coat and Obama's plan is nothing more than garden-variety communism.

The fatal flaw in Obama's new and improved Red 2.0 is the same one that visits misery on the poor souls of wretched places that have fallen into its clutches. Obama's brand of oppression must eventually suffer its only possible fate; collapse and utter failure.

In the case of the Soviet Union, it survived for the better part of the 20th Century. It survives in Red China only because those leaders have incorporated capitalism into the socialism that accompanies communism.

In Cuba it clings to life only because it has so weakened and beaten its victims that they have lapsed into the same kind of defensive ambivalence you see in the eyes of the victims of ideologically fueled starvation and subjugation in places like Darfur. They simply stop trying and opt for survival. Prosperity or even a minimal quality of life is simply not options.

There is only one way for Obama to tweak Marx's work and that is for Obama to make working compulsory. When he does, the work we will be forced to do will not be of our own choosing or even in the private sector. The right to choose one's own path and private holding of wealth are contrary to the Culture of Dependency embraced by the despotic forces now in control of Camelot that Obama vows to impose on Americans.

Obama and his thugs engage in suppression of speech, they demonize and vilify any one with the courage to stand up and confront or even question. Just ask Joe the Plumber. The Chosen One's cult is remarkably unlike their Dear Leader. He – as his running mate Joe Biden so famously said; is a "clean and articulate one." They - unwashed, inarticulate, and brutish, are his future Schutzstaffel, to be used in the continuing Kristallnacht being waged against independent thought. He pits race against race, class against class, Americans against America. (My use of German is not unintentional).

On the world stage, Barack happily promotes his plagiarism of Marx as his model for the world. In that model, America and her people are too prosperous, too under-taxed, too under controlled, *too free.*

In Obama's world, Freedom, Liberty, Justice and prosperity are things to be apportioned to those considered (by Obama) to be worthy. To achieve that end, Obama must redistribute misery and wretchedness amongst those who have risen above both. Joe the Plumber is the perfect metaphor for America, for this nation too has worked and suffered to achieve great things – an abomination in the Obamanation.

Obama was summed up nicely by the Washington Times on June 5, 2009. Writing about his disgraceful speech in Cairo during which he chastised and belittled the United States, while praising Islam (and crediting Islam with fictional advancements in science and human rights) the Times wrote:

> *"Mr. Obama's revelation of his "inner Muslim" in Cairo reveals much about who he is. He is our first president without an instinctive appreciation of the culture, history, tradition, common law and literature whence America sprang. The genetic imprint writ large in his 43 predecessors is missing from the Obama DNA.* [1]

Ask yourself this question; we know Obama's plan to divide and redistribute that which Joe the Plumber has earned (and what you and your family work for – a better life). What plan does Obama have for the division and redistribution those liberties for which America has paid in blood?

In the meantime, Obama's domestic offensive against the American way of life continues as he and his party, mount an unprecedented political Blitzkrieg against capitalism, prosperity, freedom and Americans.

---

[1] "Inner Muslim at Work in Cairo, Pruden, Jeffery, Washington Times June 5, 2009

So, what's a Tea Party and who are we?

"We hold these truths to be self-evident, that all men are created equal, that they are endowed by their Creator with certain unalienable rights, that among these are life, liberty and the pursuit of happiness. That to secure these rights, governments are instituted among men, deriving their just powers from the consent of the governed. That whenever any form of government becomes destructive to these ends, it is the right of the people to alter or to abolish it, and to institute new government, laying its foundation on such principles and organizing its powers in such form, as to them shall seem most likely to effect their safety and happiness ... all experience hath shown that mankind are more disposed to suffer, while evils are sufferable, than to right themselves by abolishing the forms to which they are accustomed. But when a long train of abuses and usurpations, pursuing invariably the same object evinces a design to reduce them under absolute despotism, it is their right, it is their duty, to throw off such government, and to provide new guards for their future security"

Thomas Jefferson, from the Declaration of Independence

We are seeing Americans living up to Jefferson's words on a grand scale. Since February 2009 there have been millions of Americans at thousands of Tea Parties. Each of them a rainbow spectrum of political views all gathering under the same banner – our Flag.

Dismissed by the political class as pawns of evil republicans and minimized by most of the media, these crowds include; pro-choicers side by side with pro-lifers; working democrats, republicans, libertarians, unaffiliated voters, blacks, whites, Latinos, Hispanics, gun rights advocates, gun control advocates… and on down the line, all gathered to defend the nation that allows them to hold and exercise those political affiliations and views.

They flood congressional "town hall meetings" with pointed questions and outrage at the lies and condescending insults they receive in response. We are called a "mob"; we are accused of creating a "manufactured" grassroots movement that they call "Astroturf.

However, those citizens at the town hall meetings and at the tea parties understand what is at stake and put aside their sometimes brutally conflicting opinions on specific issues to rise in defense of Lady Liberty.

Okay, so what is a Tea Party?

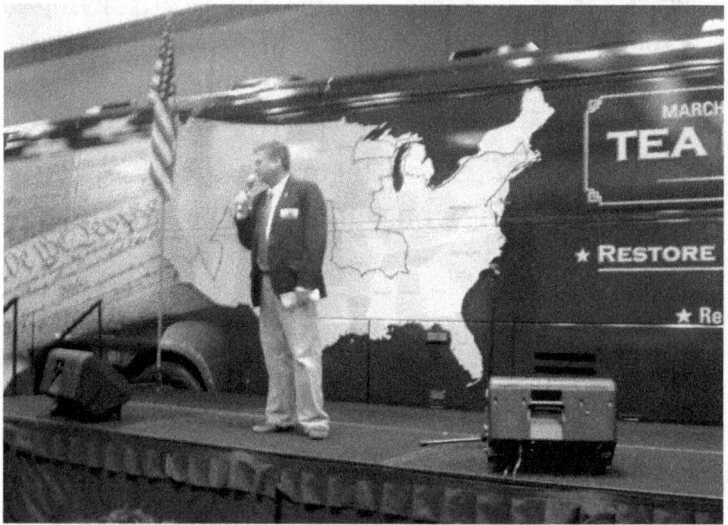

**Mark Williams leads a Tea Party Express Rally
at the California Republican 2010 convention**

Real simple. Tea Parties are gatherings of ordinary Americans, mostly middle class and middle of the road but in whole they are across the board by any measure of demographics or political leanings.

They are gatherings of people who believe in America and while maybe not knowing the Constitution verbatim nonetheless are still well schooled on its spirit, and they are gathering to Take Back America, One Tea Party at a Time.

There are literally thousands of individual Tea Party groups sporting all sorts of names but the ideas and demands remain the same from group to group.

What we do and do not Believe...

We do not believe that anybody or anything other than our Creator endows us with Human Rights and that our Constitution is a device to contain and control such government is as necessary to provide for order, the national defense and to enable the general prosperity of each of us and thus all.

The unholy forces that dare to call themselves "progressive" or "liberal" understand the Constitution to be a contrivance for thievery from those who produce in order to maintain a dependent class (themselves included) that exists by feeding off of the labor of others.

In short, Obama – Reid – Pelosi & company exist as an elite corps of parasites that send their leftovers down the food chain to those forced into dependence by programs and usury taxation created for the express purpose of being an army in waiting. This army in waiting is called into action the instant any of us begin to question affairs. They are bussed (and sometimes paid) to "protests" and given not infrequently fabricated sob stories of human suffering and misery rampant as a result of you suggesting that an effectively 50% rate of taxation may be unreasonable.

The bottom line for Tea Partiers is that we have rules for what the government may and may not do. If a rule does not exist allowing the government a particular privilege (for the advancement of all our individual Rights) then the government may not engage in that action, plain and simple.

What are the rules? That is simple too. They are *ALL* written down in the Constitution.

With that out of the way, the following are more or less the umbrella, core beliefs of the Tea Party Movement, regardless of what each group or individual may call themselves – in no particular order, differing from group to group mostly in wording but not spirit:

1. **End the bailouts**. Bailouts are simply a mechanism for the Nationalization of entire industries.

2. **Reduce the size and intrusiveness of government**. There is no Earthly reason why fulfilling the simple duties of providing for the general welfare and public defense should consume all of the national wealth well into the next, yet to born, generations. Indeed, in Obama's Administration there are no fewer than 250,000 (a quarter million!) employees who are assigned the duty of devising new and expanding old regulations and fees (taxes). Nor is there any rational reason why

the federal government should be poking around the intimate details of our lives in a perpetual effort to force us into Groupthink compliance with the Statist passion of the day.

3. **Reduce taxes.** You have heard of Tax Freedom Day? That is the first day of any given calendar year on which you have finally paid all of your federal, state, local and other taxes and fees (helpful hint: the word "fee" is a fraud, any time you are compelled to give the government wealth that you earned that is a tax regardless of what they call it.) For most of us that day falls in late May or early June, which means that we have a silent partner that cuts itself in for roughly 50-cents out of every dollar we earn (on average) and that has a voracious and insatiable appetite for more.. This is no different than being in the grip of a street gang or the Mafia, the critical difference being that the gangs and Mafia actually deliver the promised service in return.

4. **Stop the out of control spending.** It boggles one's mind to hear a parade of politicians pontificate that we must spend, borrow, and steal our way out of the hole we are in. There are legitimate government expenditures that go unaddressed for decades (hello Highway Trust Fund!) while foolish and wasteful (not to mention Unconstitutional, as in not allowed) spending ramps up daily.

5. **No health care reform**. Forgive us if we are skeptical at the very idea. After all, they have done such a splendid job with their constitutionally assigned duties (delivering the mail, defending the nation while avoiding foreign entanglements, maintaining roads, etc…) and now are pretty much destroying opportunity while propping up dead and dying business models. We'll take our chances elsewhere.

Notice that there is nothing in there about narrow or specific, lesser issues. That is why you hear howls and gnashing of teeth among the Left and their friends in the Mainstream Media. Try as they might they cannot grasp the notion of a body of people disagreeing on what a speed limit should be, or precisely what should be taught in a science class. It makes them crazy because they do not have it within them to understand Human Rights or Liberty when such are not applied according to the sanctified Groupthink dogma of the moment.

There is nothing in Tea Party doctrine compatible with the control freak mentality that is so much a part of the so-called progressive mentality, despite the emotion-laden nature of some of those lesser (in urgency, not in importance to our society).

While predominantly from a variety of Christian denominations there is nonetheless no religious aspect to the Tea Parties. Obviously we recognize the Creator that bestows rights upon us at birth and as embodied in the Constitution and there are moments of silence and prayers during the portion of our Tea Party Express shows dedicated to fallen heroes, but the events themselves have no religious affiliation.

The crowds are made up largely of current and former republicans frustrated by the party's abandonment of principle, but they also include a large number of citizens who are unaffiliated and heretofore not politically active. You will also find no shortage of democrats either, especially in Blue states like New York and Massachusetts where to not belong to the party means being isolated from the mainstream.

Should Adam marry Eve or Steve? Should little sister be forced to carry to term if she finds herself in a 'family way'? Those are just 2 questions that divide the cheering Tea Party crowds.

What unites them is their Constitutional Right to believe in and fight for their answer to each, a right they correctly understand to be under attack from the dark forces of the Left.

Similarly there have been Tea Party attendees who show up exercising their Creator bestowed right to bear arms. This nearly always results in a liberal meltdown. That is something that strikes me as particularly odd inasmuch as not infrequently the people with guns can be seen talking with and discussing – civilly – the issue of firearms with gun control advocates standing with the gun owner to protect the very same idea of Constitutional government.

Something that makes the Left even crazier, especially the media, is trying to pigeonhole and define the entire grassroots movement by assigning it a "leader."

So for all who may ask "Who is the leader of the Tea Parties?" I offer you the simple, 3-word answer to your question...

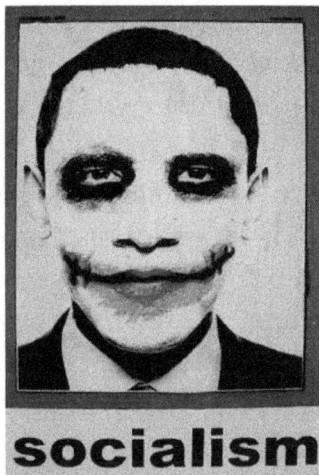

socialism

The enemy

Obama is turning out to be everything some of us feared, that he promised to be and so far, it is the only promise that he has kept. Others welcome the encroaching enslavement because it enforces their personal limits on us all.

Barack Obama and his followers embody the Seven Deadly Sins; pride, greed, envy, wrath, lust, gluttony and sloth.

The man and those around and allied with him are driven by a narcissistic pride that allows no room for being wrong in his worldview, nor does it allow room for facts to derail his increasing, angry determination to not be disputed. He and his kind derive power from the exploitation and feeding of his followers' envy, greed, sloth, and gluttony. Where the President deviates from garden-variety liberalism and ventures deep into the depravity of authoritarian socialism is the sin of wrath.

Secretary of Homeland Security Janet Napolitano and the administration for which she works dismisses Muslim terrorists as ordinary criminals, while taking great pains to warn of what she sees as the sinister and immediate threat posed to the Homeland by; our heroic veterans, our police (and all others who have reaffirmed their Oaths to uphold and protect the Constitution), Tea Partiers and grandma attempting to pass through airport "security" on her way to visit the grandkids.

The Speaker of the United States House of Representatives has labeled patriotic citizens Nazis and racists.

Harry Reid, the President of the United States Senate calls them "mobs" ginned up by insurance companies and the Republican Party.

President Obama is becoming ever more belligerent and in a pair of actions that when taken side by side add "frightening" to his titles as he persists in confusing his welfare thug background with leadership. We sit in horror watching him replace constitutional processes with that thuggery, and bribes, payoffs and outright criminal behavior in order to not be denied his passion, to destroy the United States as a guardian of individual Human Rights.

It is President Obama who admitted knowing nothing of the arrest of a black Harvard professor by a white Cambridge police officer during a disturbance but then went on to say that the police acted "stupidly." Yet when a Muslim Jihadist sleeper terrorist shot 13 soldiers at Fort Hood Texas that same president, after being informed of all the details went public several days after the fact and instructed us all to "avoid rushing to conclusions" about the nature of the crime..

His words and those of Pelosi, Reid and the unions convey the clear message that there is a very real incitement to violence against Americans. The presidential tone is increasingly arrogant and mean as he struggles to cram the socialist agenda down our throats, including the nationalization of entire industries critical to our prosperity and power. We are witness to nothing less than a revolution in which a powerful insurgency seeks to overturn the one and only guardian of Human Rights on Earth and replace our system with one of Third World wretchedness for the masses and favoritism for the ruling elite.

I told my radio audiences in 2008 that the election that November could very well be the last free election in our brief history if Barack Obama won. He won and in just his first few months in office has managed to all but outlaw opposition and is well on his way to criminalizing dissenting opinion.

We must continue to resist this evil agenda and fight back as vigorously as if we were at war and repelling a foreign invasion... because that is really what we are facing.

When opposition candidates or people like me start going to jail, it will be too late, but because of the Tea Parties, and Patriots like you I feel confident that the Union will stand well and strong, and that our enemies both domestic and foreign *will* be defeated.

Not on our watch, not here, not ever.

Learn more and follow my daily updates from the front lines of the War for America's Soul

at

www.MarkTalk.com

Write to me: mark@marktalk.com

And follow the Tea Party Express at
www.TeaPartyExpress.org

Appendix 1
America's owners manual

Constitution of the United States

We the People of the United States, in Order to form a more perfect Union, establish Justice, insure domestic Tranquility, provide for the common defense, promote the general Welfare, and secure the Blessings of Liberty to ourselves and our Posterity, do ordain and establish this Constitution for the United States of America.

Article I

Section 1

All legislative Powers herein granted shall be vested in a Congress of the United States, which shall consist of a Senate and House of Representatives.

Section 2

The House of Representatives shall be composed of Members chosen every second Year by the People of the several States, and the Electors in each State shall have the Qualifications requisite for Electors of the most numerous Branch of the State Legislature.

No Person shall be a Representative who shall not have attained to the Age of twenty five Years, and been seven Years a Citizen of the United States, and who shall not, when elected, be an Inhabitant of that State in which he shall be chosen.

Representatives and direct Taxes shall be apportioned among the several States which may be included within this Union, according to their respective Numbers, which shall be determined by adding to the whole Number of free Persons, including those bound to Service for a Term of Years, and excluding Indians not taxed, three fifths of all other Persons. The actual Enumeration shall be made within three Years after the first Meeting of the Congress of the United States, and within every subsequent Term of ten Years, in such Manner as they shall by Law direct. The Number of Representatives shall not exceed one for every thirty Thousand, but each State shall have at Least one Representative; and until such enumeration shall be made, the State of New Hampshire shall be entitled to chuse three, Massachusetts eight, Rhode-Island and Providence Plantations one, Connecticut five, New-York six, New Jersey four, Pennsylvania eight, Delaware one, Maryland six, Virginia ten, North Carolina five, South Carolina five, and Georgia three.

When vacancies happen in the Representation from any State, the Executive Authority thereof shall issue Writs of Election to fill such Vacancies.

The House of Representatives shall chuse their Speaker and other Officers; and shall have the sole Power of Impeachment.

Section 3

The Senate of the United States shall be composed of two Senators from each State, chosen by the Legislature thereof for six Years; and each Senator shall have one Vote.

Immediately after they shall be assembled in Consequence of the first Election, they shall be divided as equally as may be into three Classes. The Seats of the Senators of the first Class shall be vacated at the Expiration of the second Year, of the second Class at the Expiration of the fourth Year, and of the third Class at the Expiration of the sixth Year, so that one third may be chosen every second Year; and if Vacancies happen by Resignation, or otherwise, during the Recess of the Legislature of any State, the Executive thereof may make temporary Appointments until the next Meeting of the Legislature, which shall then fill such Vacancies.

No Person shall be a Senator who shall not have attained to the Age of thirty Years, and been nine Years a Citizen of the United States, and who shall not, when elected, be an Inhabitant of that State for which he shall be chosen.

The Vice President of the United States shall be President of the Senate, but shall have no Vote, unless they be equally divided.

The Senate shall chuse their other Officers, and also a President pro tempore, in the Absence of the Vice President, or when he shall exercise the Office of President of the United States.

The Senate shall have the sole Power to try all Impeachments. When sitting for that Purpose, they shall be on Oath or Affirmation. When the President of the United States is tried, the Chief Justice shall preside: And no Person shall be convicted without the Concurrence of two thirds of the Members present.

Judgment in Cases of Impeachment shall not extend further than to removal from Office, and disqualification to hold and enjoy any Office of honor, Trust or Profit under the United States: but the

Party convicted shall nevertheless be liable and subject to Indictment, Trial, Judgment and Punishment, according to Law.

Section. 4

The Times, Places and Manner of holding Elections for Senators and Representatives, shall be prescribed in each State by the Legislature thereof; but the Congress may at any time by Law make or alter such Regulations, except as to the Places of chusing Senators.

The Congress shall assemble at least once in every Year, and such Meeting shall be on the first Monday in December, unless they shall by Law appoint a different Day.

Section 5

Each House shall be the Judge of the Elections, Returns and Qualifications of its own Members, and a Majority of each shall constitute a Quorum to do Business; but a smaller Number may adjourn from day to day, and may be authorized to compel the Attendance of absent Members, in such Manner, and under such Penalties as each House may provide.

Each House may determine the Rules of its Proceedings, punish its Members for disorderly Behaviour, and, with the Concurrence of two thirds, expel a Member.

Each House shall keep a Journal of its Proceedings, and from time to time publish the same, excepting such Parts as may in their Judgment require Secrecy; and the Yeas and Nays of the Members of either House on any question shall, at the Desire of one fifth of those Present, be entered on the Journal.

Neither House, during the Session of Congress, shall, without the Consent of the other, adjourn for more than three days, nor to any other Place than that in which the two Houses shall be sitting.

Section 6

The Senators and Representatives shall receive a Compensation for their Services, to be ascertained by Law, and paid out of the Treasury of the United States. They shall in all Cases, except Treason, Felony and Breach of the Peace, be privileged from Arrest during their Attendance at the Session of their respective Houses, and in going to and returning from the same; and for any Speech or Debate in either House, they shall not be questioned in any other Place.

No Senator or Representative shall, during the Time for which he was elected, be appointed to any civil Office under the Authority of the United States, which shall have been created, or the Emoluments whereof shall have been encreased during such time; and no Person holding any Office under the United States, shall be a Member of either House during his Continuance in Office.

Section 7

All Bills for raising Revenue shall originate in the House of Representatives; but the Senate may propose or concur with Amendments as on other Bills.

Every Bill which shall have passed the House of Representatives and the Senate, shall, before it become a Law, be presented to the President of the United States: If he approve he shall sign it, but if not he shall return it, with his Objections to that House in which it shall have originated, who shall enter the Objections at large on their Journal, and proceed to reconsider it.If after such Reconsideration two thirds of that House shall agree to pass the Bill, it shall be sent, together with the Objections, to the other House, by which it shall likewise be reconsidered, and if approved by two thirds of that House, it shall become a Law. But in all such Cases the Votes of both Houses shall be determined by yeas and Nays, and the Names of the Persons voting for and against the Bill shall be entered on the Journal of each House respectively. If any Bill shall not be returned by the President within ten Days (Sundays excepted) after it shall have been presented to him, the Same shall be a Law, in like Manner as if he had signed it, unless the Congress by their Adjournment prevent its Return, in which Case it shall not be a Law.

Every Order, Resolution, or Vote to which the Concurrence of the Senate and House of Representatives may be necessary (except on a question of Adjournment) shall be presented to the President of the United States; and before the Same shall take Effect, shall be approved by him, or being disapproved by him, shall be repassed by two thirds of the Senate and House of Representatives, according to the Rules and Limitations prescribed in the Case of a Bill.

Section 8

The Congress shall have Power To lay and collect Taxes, Duties, Imposts and Excises, to pay the Debts and provide for the common Defence and general Welfare of the United States; but all Duties, Imposts and Excises shall be uniform throughout the United States;

To borrow Money on the credit of the United States;

To regulate Commerce with foreign Nations, and among the several States, and with the Indian Tribes;

To establish an uniform Rule of Naturalization, and uniform Laws on the subject of Bankruptcies throughout the United States;

To coin Money, regulate the Value thereof, and of foreign Coin, and fix the Standard of Weights and Measures;

To provide for the Punishment of counterfeiting the Securities and current Coin of the United States;

To establish Post Offices and post Roads;

To promote the Progress of Science and useful Arts, by securing for limited Times to Authors and Inventors the exclusive Right to their respective Writings and Discoveries;

To constitute Tribunals inferior to the supreme Court;

To define and punish Piracies and Felonies committed on the high Seas, and Offences against the Law of Nations;

To declare War, grant Letters of Marque and Reprisal, and make Rules concerning Captures on Land and Water;

To raise and support Armies, but no Appropriation of Money to that Use shall be for a longer Term than two Years;

To provide and maintain a Navy;

To make Rules for the Government and Regulation of the land and naval Forces;

To provide for calling forth the Militia to execute the Laws of the Union, suppress Insurrections and repel Invasions;

To provide for organizing, arming, and disciplining, the Militia, and for governing such Part of them as may be employed in the Service of the United States, reserving to the States respectively, the Appointment of the Officers, and the Authority of training the Militia according to the discipline prescribed by Congress;

To exercise exclusive Legislation in all Cases whatsoever, over such District (not exceeding ten Miles square) as may, by Cession of particular States, and the Acceptance of Congress, become the Seat

of the Government of the United States, and to exercise like Authority over all Places purchased by the Consent of the Legislature of the State in which the Same shall be, for the Erection of Forts, Magazines, Arsenals, dock-Yards, and other needful Buildings;--And

To make all Laws which shall be necessary and proper for carrying into Execution the foregoing Powers, and all other Powers vested by this Constitution in the Government of the United States, or in any Department or Officer thereof.

Section 9

The Migration or Importation of such Persons as any of the States now existing shall think proper to admit, shall not be prohibited by the Congress prior to the Year one thousand eight hundred and eight, but a Tax or duty may be imposed on such Importation, not exceeding ten dollars for each Person.

The Privilege of the Writ of Habeas Corpus shall not be suspended, unless when in Cases of Rebellion or Invasion the public Safety may require it.

No Bill of Attainder or ex post facto Law shall be passed.

No Capitation, or other direct, Tax shall be laid, unless in Proportion to the Census or enumeration herein before directed to be taken.

No Tax or Duty shall be laid on Articles exported from any State.

No Preference shall be given by any Regulation of Commerce or Revenue to the Ports of one State over those of another; nor shall Vessels bound to, or from, one State, be obliged to enter, clear, or pay Duties in another.

No Money shall be drawn from the Treasury, but in Consequence of Appropriations made by Law; and a regular Statement and Account of the Receipts and Expenditures of all public Money shall be published from time to time.

No Title of Nobility shall be granted by the United States: And no Person holding any Office of Profit or Trust under them, shall, without the Consent of the Congress, accept of any present, Emolument, Office, or Title, of any kind whatever, from any King, Prince, or foreign State.

Section 10

No State shall enter into any Treaty, Alliance, or Confederation; grant Letters of Marque and Reprisal; coin Money; emit Bills of Credit; make any Thing but gold and silver Coin a Tender in Payment of Debts; pass any Bill of Attainder, ex post facto Law, or Law impairing the Obligation of Contracts, or grant any Title of Nobility.

No State shall, without the Consent of the Congress, lay any Imposts or Duties on Imports or Exports, except what may be absolutely necessary for executing it's inspection Laws: and the net Produce of

all Duties and Imposts, laid by any State on Imports or Exports, shall be for the Use of the Treasury of the United States; and all such Laws shall be subject to the Revision and Controul of the Congress.

No State shall, without the Consent of Congress, lay any Duty of Tonnage, keep Troops, or Ships of War in time of Peace, enter into any Agreement or Compact with another State, or with a foreign

Power, or engage in War, unless actually invaded, or in such imminent Danger as will not admit of delay.

Article II

Section 1

The executive Power shall be vested in a President of the United States of America. He shall hold his Office during the Term of four Years, and, together with the Vice President, chosen for the same Term, be elected, as follows:

Each State shall appoint, in such Manner as the Legislature thereof may direct, a Number of Electors, equal to the whole Number of Senators and Representatives to which the State may be entitled in the Congress: but no Senator or Representative, or Person holding an Office of Trust or Profit under the United States, shall be appointed an Elector.

The Electors shall meet in their respective States, and vote by Ballot for two Persons, of whom one at least shall not be an Inhabitant of the same State with themselves. And they shall make a List of all the Persons voted for, and of the Number of Votes for each; which List they shall sign and certify, and transmit sealed to the Seat of the

Government of the United States, directed to the President of the Senate. The President of the Senate shall, in the Presence of the Senate and House of Representatives, open all the Certificates, and the Votes shall then be counted. The Person having the greatest

Number of Votes shall be the President, if such Number be a Majority of the whole Number of Electors appointed; and if there be more than one who have such Majority, and have an equal Number of Votes, then the House of Representatives shall immediately chuse by Ballot one of them for President; and if no Person have a Majority, then from the five highest on the List the said House shall in like Manner chuse the President. But in chusing the President, the

Votes shall be taken by States, the Representation from each State having one Vote; A quorum for this purpose shall consist of a Member or Members from two thirds of the States, and a Majority of all the States shall be necessary to a Choice. In every Case, after the Choice of the President, the Person having the greatest Number of

Votes of the Electors shall be the Vice President. But if there should remain two or more who have equal Votes, the Senate shall chuse from them by Ballot the Vice President.

The Congress may determine the Time of chusing the Electors, and the Day on which they shall give their Votes; which Day shall be the same throughout the United States.

No Person except a natural born Citizen, or a Citizen of the United States, at the time of the Adoption of this Constitution, shall be eligible to the Office of President; neither shall any Person be eligible to that Office who shall not have attained to the Age of thirty five Years, and been fourteen Years a Resident within the United States.

In Case of the Removal of the President from Office, or of his Death, Resignation, or Inability to discharge the Powers and Duties of the said Office, the Same shall devolve on the Vice President, and the Congress may by Law provide for the Case of Removal, Death, Resignation or Inability, both of the President and Vice President, declaring what Officer shall then act as President, and such Officer

shall act accordingly, until the Disability be removed, or a President shall be elected.

The President shall, at stated Times, receive for his Services, a Compensation, which shall neither be increased nor diminished during the Period for which he shall have been elected, and he shall not receive within that Period any other Emolument from the United States, or any of them.

Before he enter on the Execution of his Office, he shall take the following Oath or Affirmation:--"I do solemnly swear (or affirm) that I will faithfully execute the Office of President of the United States, and will to the best of my Ability, preserve, protect and defend the Constitution of the United States."

Section 2

The President shall be Commander in Chief of the Army and Navy of the United States, and of the Militia of the several States, when called into the actual Service of the United States; he may require the Opinion, in writing, of the principal Officer in each of the executive Departments, upon any Subject relating to the Duties of their respective Offices, and he shall have Power to grant Reprieves and Pardons for Offences against the United States, except in Cases of Impeachment.

He shall have Power, by and with the Advice and Consent of the Senate, to make Treaties, provided two thirds of the Senators present concur; and he shall nominate, and by and with the Advice and Consent of the Senate, shall appoint Ambassadors, other public Ministers and Consuls, Judges of the supreme Court, and all other Officers of the United States, whose Appointments are not herein otherwise provided for, and which shall be established by Law: but the Congress may by Law vest the Appointment of such inferior Officers, as they think proper, in the President alone, in the Courts of Law, or in the Heads of Departments.

The President shall have Power to fill up all Vacancies that may happen during the Recess of the Senate, by granting Commissions which shall expire at the End of their next Session.

Section 3

He shall from time to time give to the Congress Information of the State of the Union, and recommend to their Consideration such Measures as he shall judge necessary and expedient; he may, on extraordinary Occasions, convene both Houses, or either of them, and in Case of Disagreement between them, with Respect to the Time of Adjournment, he may adjourn them to such Time as he shall think proper; he shall receive Ambassadors and other public Ministers; he shall take Care that the Laws be faithfully executed, and shall Commission all the Officers of the United States.

Section 4

The President, Vice President and all civil Officers of the United States, shall be removed from Office on Impeachment for, and Conviction of, Treason, Bribery, or other high Crimes and Misdemeanors.

Article III

Section 1

The judicial Power of the United States shall be vested in one supreme Court, and in such inferior Courts as the Congress may from time to time ordain and establish. The Judges, both of the supreme and inferior Courts, shall hold their Offices during good Behaviour, and shall, at stated Times, receive for their Services a Compensation, which shall not be diminished during their Continuance in Office.

Section 2

The judicial Power shall extend to all Cases, in Law and Equity, arising under this Constitution, the Laws of the United States, and

Treaties made, or which shall be made, under their Authority;--to all Cases affecting Ambassadors, other public Ministers and Consuls;--to all Cases of admiralty and maritime Jurisdiction;--to Controversies to which the United States shall be a Party;--to Controversies between two or more States;-- between a State and Citizens of another State,-- between Citizens of different States,--between Citizens of the same State claiming Lands under Grants of different States, and between a State, or the Citizens thereof, and foreign States, Citizens or Subjects.

In all Cases affecting Ambassadors, other public Ministers and Consuls, and those in which a State shall be Party, the supreme Court shall have original Jurisdiction. In all the other Cases before mentioned, the supreme Court shall have appellate Jurisdiction, both as to Law and Fact, with such Exceptions, and under such Regulations as the Congress shall make.

The Trial of all Crimes, except in Cases of Impeachment, shall be by Jury; and such Trial shall be held in the State where the said Crimes shall have been committed; but when not committed within any State, the Trial shall be at such Place or Places as the Congress may by Law have directed.

Section 3

Treason against the United States, shall consist only in levying War against them, or in adhering to their Enemies, giving them Aid and Comfort. No Person shall be convicted of Treason unless on the Testimony of two Witnesses to the same overt Act, or on Confession in open Court.

The Congress shall have Power to declare the Punishment of
Treason, but no Attainder of Treason shall work Corruption of
Blood, or Forfeiture except during the Life of the Person attainted.

Article IV

Section 1

Full Faith and Credit shall be given in each State to the public Acts,
Records, and judicial Proceedings of every other State. And the
Congress may by general Laws prescribe the Manner in which such
Acts, Records and Proceedings shall be proved, and the Effect
thereof.

Section 2

The Citizens of each State shall be entitled to all Privileges and
Immunities of Citizens in the several States.

A Person charged in any State with Treason, Felony, or other Crime,
who shall flee from Justice, and be found in another State, shall on
Demand of the executive Authority of the State from which he fled,
be delivered up, to be removed to the State having Jurisdiction of the
Crime.

No Person held to Service or Labour in one State, under the Laws
thereof, escaping into another, shall, in Consequence of any Law or
Regulation therein, be discharged from such Service or Labour, but
shall be delivered up on Claim of the Party to whom such Service or
Labour may be due.

Section 3

New States may be admitted by the Congress into this Union; but no
new State shall be formed or erected within the Jurisdiction of any
other State; nor any State be formed by the Junction of two or more

States, or Parts of States, without the Consent of the Legislatures of the States concerned as well as of the Congress.

The Congress shall have Power to dispose of and make all needful Rules and Regulations respecting the Territory or other Property

belonging to the United States; and nothing in this Constitution shall be so construed as to Prejudice any Claims of the United States, or of any particular State.

Section 4

The United States shall guarantee to every State in this Union a Republican Form of Government, and shall protect each of them against Invasion; and on Application of the Legislature, or of the Executive (when the Legislature cannot be convened), against domestic Violence.

Article V

The Congress, whenever two thirds of both Houses shall deem it necessary, shall propose Amendments to this Constitution, or, on the Application of the Legislatures of two thirds of the several States, shall call a Convention for proposing Amendments, which, in either Case, shall be valid to all Intents and Purposes, as Part of this Constitution, when ratified by the Legislatures of three fourths of the several States, or by Conventions in three fourths thereof, as the one or the other Mode of Ratification may be proposed by the Congress; Provided that no Amendment which may be made prior to the Year One thousand eight hundred and eight shall in any Manner affect the first and fourth Clauses in the Ninth Section of the first Article; and that no State, without its Consent, shall be deprived of its equal Suffrage in the Senate.

Article VI

All Debts contracted and Engagements entered into, before the Adoption of this Constitution, shall be as valid against the United States under this Constitution, as under the Confederation.

This Constitution, and the Laws of the United States which shall be made in Pursuance thereof; and all Treaties made, or which shall be made, under the Authority of the United States, shall be the supreme Law of the Land; and the Judges in every State shall be bound thereby, any Thing in the Constitution or Laws of any State to the Contrary notwithstanding.

The Senators and Representatives before mentioned, and the Members of the several State Legislatures, and all executive and judicial Officers, both of the United States and of the several States, shall be bound by Oath or Affirmation, to support this Constitution; but no religious Test shall ever be required as a Qualification to any Office or public Trust under the United States

[Author's note: For the final Article VII (dealing with the ratification of this document) the signatories and amendments 11 – 27 please visit the National Constitution Center on line – referenced on page 185. And the Constitution has been amended 27 times since it was written and ratified. Those changes are not reflected in this appendix. Please visit the National Constitution Center at www.constitutioncenter.org to learn more about America's owners manual]

Appendix 2
Your Bill of Rights

First Amendment – Establishment Clause, Free Exercise Clause; freedom of speech, of the press, Freedom of Religion, and of assembly; right to petition,

Congress shall make no law respecting an establishment of religion, or prohibiting the free exercise thereof; or abridging the freedom of speech, or of the press; or the right of the people peaceably to assemble, and to petition the Government for a redress of grievances.

Second Amendment – Right to keep and bear arms.

A well regulated Militia, being necessary to the security of a free State, the right of the People to keep and bear Arms, shall not be infringed. [5][6]

Third Amendment – Protection from quartering of troops.

No Soldier shall, in time of peace be quartered in any house, without the consent of the Owner, nor in time of war, but in a manner to be prescribed by law.

Fourth Amendment – Protection from unreasonable search and seizure.

The right of the people to be secure in their persons, houses, papers, and effects, against unreasonable searches and seizures, shall not be violated, and no Warrants shall issue, but upon probable cause, supported by Oath or affirmation, and particularly describing the place to be searched, and the persons or things to be seized.

Fifth Amendment – due process, double jeopardy, self-incrimination, eminent domain.

No person shall be held to answer for any capital, or otherwise infamous crime, unless on a presentment or indictment of a Grand Jury, except in cases arising in the land or naval forces, or in the Militia, when in actual service in time of War or public danger; nor shall any person be subject for the same offence to be twice put in jeopardy of life or limb; nor shall be compelled in any criminal case to be a witness against himself, nor be deprived of life, liberty, or property, without due process of law; nor shall private property be taken for public use, without just compensation.

Sixth Amendment – Trial by jury and rights of the accused; Confrontation Clause, speedy trial, public trial, right to counsel

In all criminal prosecutions, the accused shall enjoy the right to a speedy and public trial, by an impartial jury of the State and district

where in the crime shall have been committed, which district shall have been previously ascertained by law, and to be informed of the nature and cause of the accusation; to be confronted with the witnesses against him; to have compulsory process for obtaining witnesses in his favor, and to have the Assistance of Counsel for his defense.

Seventh Amendment – Civil trial by jury.

In suits at common law, where the value in controversy shall exceed twenty dollars, the right of trial by jury shall be preserved, and no fact tried by a jury, shall be otherwise re-examined in any court of the United States, than according to the rules of the common law.

Eighth Amendment – Prohibition of excessive bail and cruel and unusual punishment.

Excessive bail shall not be required, nor excessive fines imposed, nor cruel and unusual punishments inflicted.

Ninth Amendment – Protection of rights not specifically enumerated in the Bill of Rights.

The enumeration in the Constitution, of certain rights, shall not be construed to deny or disparage others retained by the people.

Tenth Amendment – Powers of States and people.

The powers not delegated to the United States by the Constitution, nor prohibited by it to the States, are reserved to the States respectively, or to the people.

God Bless & protect America

www.ingramcontent.com/pod-product-compliance
Lightning Source LLC
Chambersburg PA
CBHW031511270326
41930CB00006B/354